As an administrator for the Canadian Pr[...] number of seminars and other education[...] deal with in your book, but nothing as c[...] have developed... I believe that "Golf: The Mind-Body Co[...] help any golfer interested in improving their game, but will be of particular assistance to higher level players who have aspirations of competing at the national or international level in golf.

Bob Beauchemin, Past Commissioner ' Canadian Professional Golf Tour

I believe that Dr. Saunders' program represents a true breakthrough for the serious golfer interested in conquering the mental side of golf."

Jennifer Keiver, Women's Professional Golfers European Tour,
Professional Golfers Association

Few people understand how important mental preparation is for game improvement and self satisfaction. This program is truly a tool for improving your game. It allows a beginner to understand mental preparation at a level equal to his early skill level. A low handicap player or professional can use the same information to expand knowledge of himself and to practice his mental game. The golf professional can provide instruction and some mental prparation, but there is still a void. Dr. Saunders program Golf: The Mind-Body Connection is the answer to that void.

Lloyd A. McBean, C.P.G.A., Director of Golf, Lakeside Greens Golf & Country Club

I have incorporated your principles in the past with modest success. With your recent edition of Golf: The Mind-Body Connection, I personally discovered another level of possibility for myself.- It is almost as if I am in an altered state with a sense of beginning wizardry showing up at my doorstep as I refresh my experience with the game of golf.

Philip Perry, Ph.D. Sport Psychologist

This book delivers! After spending years working on my game, and many hours on the practice range, I felt I had learned a lot about how to swing a golf club. However, whenever I had a good round going I would somehow blow up and ruin my score, usually a result of nerves! Dr. Saunders book turned out to be just what I needed. His soothing voice on the Cds helped me to reach a state of relaxation that was easy to recall on the course. As a direct result, I won first place in the first flight of my club championship within three weeks of practiing his method. My handicap went down 5 strokes from 13 to an 8. Now when I feel the nerves I am able to utilize his technique and my performance actually improves rather than falls apart like it used to. I am currently a 5 handicap. I stongly recommend this book.

J.P Perreault, Houston TX.

I bought your book about a year ago from Amazon.com. I have played many sports and therefore when I took up golf a year and a half ago I knew that I would have to work on the mental side. Your book has been fantastic in this regard. I only wish I had had access to your techniques when I played cricket competitively. - I set myself an ambitious goal of getting to single figures by this June (after playing for 1.5 years). I started at 24 and am now down to a 10 handicap. Interestingly I stopped practicing the mental side as there has been more technical things to work on as my handicap has approached single figures. Consequently I have seen my handicap begin an upward trend. For this reason I am planning to spend more time on the mental side of the game. . . (A recent e-mail indicates that Stephen is now down to an 8 handicap.)

Stephen Newton (Via e-mail)

GOLF
THE MIND-BODY
CONNECTION

GOLF
THE MIND-BODY
CONNECTION

How To Lower Your Score With Mental Training

T.C. SAUNDERS, M.D.

Canadian Cataloguing in Publication Data

Saunders, T.C. (Thomas Campbell.) 1921 -
Golf: the mind-body connection [kit]: how to lower your score with mental training
Originally published. under title: Inner mental training for golf.
Includes bibliographical references, index
ISBN 1 - 895310-03-2

1. Golf–Psychological aspects. 2. Golf–Training
I. Mind-Body Golf Ltd. II. Title. III. Title: Inner mental training for golf.

GV979.P75S39 1997 796.352'01'9 C97-0900146-3

Published by: Mind-Body Golf
                105 Sierra Morena Terrace SW
                Calgary, Alberta, Canada, T3H 3A2

Printed in Canada
second printing 2001, with minor revisions.

Type set and graphics: desnoyers-schuler inc., communicating by design
Cover design: Karol Fodor, Digital Art
Original music: EK Sound
Compact disc recording: Jason Wright, Dark Matter Productions
Editor: Tim Cornish

DISCLAIMER

In view of the complex nature of individuals, their unique medical or psychological problems and the complexities of the game of golf, this program is not intended to replace professional medical, psychological, or golf advice. The author and publisher expressly disclaim any responsibility for any liability, loss, or risk, personal or otherwise which is incurred as a consequence, directly or indirectly of the use and application of any of this program.

TO MY FAMILY

T a b l e   o f   C o n t e n t s

Listen to the introduction (track 1 of disc 1) and do Exercise 1a on relaxation (track 2 of disc 1) after reading this chapter.

Exercises 1a and 1b (tracks 2 and 3 of disc 1) fit with this chapter. Exercise 1a is for learning, Exercise 1b for practice until you are familiar enough to do the PMR exercise on your own.

Exercise 2 (track 4 of disc 1) belongs with this chapter. Set aside 30 minutes in a quiet place to do this exercise, the longest of all the exercises.

Exercises 3, 4, 5, and 6 (tracks 1 through 4 of disc 2) are all concerned with developing your concentration skills. They belong with this and the next chapter. They are short exercises and could be done as a break in your reading of these two chapters.

Exercise 7 (track 5 of disc 2) belongs with this chapter. You should read the chapter before doing the exercise because it includes description of a biofeedback experiment which you will do during the exercise.

There is no one exercise devoted to imaging goals being achieved. Rather, I have suggested that you do this very important imagery in several of the exercises.

Exercises 8 and 9 (tracks 6 and 7 of disc 2) are simulation exercises to practice these techniques in your mind before you have to use them in real life.

Exercise 10 (track 8 of disc 2) is a simulation of the technique to first recall, and then to project into a future game, the feelings that accompany a peak performance.

A c k n o w l e d g e m e n t s

This new, completely revised edition of Mind-Body Golf© is now entitled Golf: The Mind-Body Connection. It contains new and important information. The exercises are narrated on two compact discs for easier access to individual exercises.

I would like to thank the people who gave freely of their time and energy to read the manuscript and offer constructive suggestions for this edition. John Dawson, Tait McPhedran, Don and Carolyn Larsen, Francis Lodato, Elizabeth Van der Wee (she also recorded the introduction on the CDs), and Joan Hudson all made very helpful editing suggestions. Bob Pratt, Don Repka, Gayle Marshall, Al Krebs, Pat Hutchinson, and Barry Flavelle read the manuscript in its early stages and provided encouragement. Carson Manzer made sure that the writing of Appendix One was correct and clearly described his diary concept. Philip Perry, who introduced me to Lars Eric Uneståhl, read the manuscript in its final stage. He offered valuable, constructive ideas which have been incorporated into the final product. Thanks to my editor Tim Cornish for his enthusiasm and for the expertise he brought to the project. Particular thanks to Cliff Rowell of Hands-On Graphics for his help with the production of the book.

F o r e w o r d

Those of you who are familiar with my attitude toward recorded presentations may be surprised to find me endorsing Golf: The Mind-Body Connection. Few if any recorded presentations help the golfer achieve the goals these programs set out to achieve. Dr. Saunders work, on the other hand, keeps it simple and helps the golfer understand the methods implicit in mental preparation. His clear, gentle approach to concentration and goal setting demonstrates his years of clinical and golf experience. His successes at improving his own game and at testing and applying these techniques are evident throughout the text.

This work by Dr. Tom Saunders is different. It does not promise you the moon, nor does it give you the impression that there is a sleeping giant within that, once awakened, will transform you into a scratch golfer. It does, on the other hand, offer you sound, scientifically-tested ways and means to perform better at golf while enjoying it more. Dr. Saunders not only motivates, but teaches. He does not assume, he explains. He encourages and guides his audience toward improving not only their golf game, but their personal lives. Furthermore, Golf: The Mind-Body Connection, provides the means to achieve the goals set forth in the program.

It is difficult to assess adequately how much of any sport is mental. However, regardless of what that percentage is, be it ten percent or fifty percent, the golfer who does not do some properly conceived and scientifically-tested mental preparation is not fully prepared to play. This is as true for the professional on tour as it is for the weekend warrior. Dr. Saunders patiently and insightfully presents the ways and means by which any golfer may learn mental preparation.

Remember as you read that Dr. Saunders program will not bring your game from 100 to par. Honestly, he doesn't ever pretend to be able to do this. What he attempts to do is to help you concentrate and enjoy the game more, and change frustration to satisfaction.

I have seen this work grow from its earliest stages. The painstaking attention to detail that Dr. Saunders has brought to this work makes it a must for anyone who is serious about mental preparation. Golf: The Mind-Body Connection will bring a wonderfully practical perspective to your game.

I have introduced Dr. Saunders' work to all of my golf clients and friends. I am sure that you will enjoy the program as much as I have.

Francis J. Lodato, Ph.D., ABPP,

Sport Psychologist to the

Calgary Stampeders Football Club,

the *Los Angeles Kings* (until 1994),

and to various college teams.

I n t r o d u c t i o n

*". . . this much is certain: golf is a game in which
attitude of mind counts for incomparably
more than mightiness of muscle."*

Arnold Haultain, 1908

This program began in 1989 when there were few mental training programs available for the average golfer. Books and videos outlined the psychological aspects of golf, but the person was then left with the difficult task of making that knowledge a part of his or her mental skills for playing golf. This program combines a source book which outlines the theories and techniques for developing your Inner Mental Skills, then provides you the means (recorded exercises) to make that knowledge a part of your mental state for playing better golf.

The game of golf draws you into the present moment, playing the shot that faces you and playing that shot to the best of your ability. When you experience the flowing concentration of good golf, you will not be hung up on the memory of errant shots, nor will you be telling yourself *what not to do with the shot.*

Golf: The Mind-Body Connection gives you a quick and efficient method to avoid these pitfalls. You will discover how easy it is to have an achievable state of confidence for better shot-making. You will learn to be positive about your game and to expect to play well. Enjoyment of the game will increase as you improve your scores.

Our dominant everyday mental activity is logical, sequential, analytic problem solving. Performance in sport requires achieving the right level of relaxation, using imagery in creative ways and focusing on the present to the exclusion of all else. These are basic Inner Mental Skills, the skills which allow you to better learn, to hone your swing, and to increase your enjoyment of the game of golf.

The goals of this program are:

When you have absorbed the contents of the book, and mastered the exercises on the compact discs, you will be able to:

- quickly achieve a state of active relaxation (the balanced relaxation that comes with good performance)

- use mental imagery to learn and improve your golf game

- develop positive thoughts and behavior patterns for your golf game

- focus completely on the shot you are about to make

- recall images of a peak (or best) performance, and project the associated feelings into the image of each shot of an upcoming game

Chapter one
Inner mental
training

"If my mind can conceive it, and I can believe it,
I then can achieve it."

Larry Holmes

● The Mental Game

Golf can be an exhilarating game when you are playing well, but it can be frustrating and difficult when you play poorly. When the poor play continues with only a few good shots to relieve the frustration, you can become angry at yourself, angry at golf. Aside from anger, a range of emotions can get in the way of good performance in golf. The first tee jitters, when you have to perform in front of other people, is common. Or, when playing well and wanting to make your best score ever, you start to feel victorious too soon in the game and the fear of missing putts takes over. Unfortunately, as you try hard to get rid of the fears, errors magnify and these negative emotions can intensify.

The mind and the body are very closely connected. How we think of ourselves, that is, the image we have of ourselves, affects the way our body systems function. When body systems do not function at their best, performance suffers. At its worst, this exemplifies another premise of Golf: The Mind-Body Connection: that some emotions and negative thoughts and images of yourself can produce poor performance.

For a tour player, just like an Olympian, the difference between winning and losing lies in mental preparation. Jack Nicklaus is quoted as saying that golf is 90 percent a mental game. It is difficult to assign a percentage like this for an average golfer whose golf skills are not as well grooved as are Jack's. Nevertheless, the mental aspects of the game are enormously important for learning and honing your golf shots. Until recent years, the Western World had few books or other programs on how to master the mental problems that are a part of golf.

● Self-Hypnosis

Reading about the mental training that Olympians were practicing, I was struck by the similarity with what I was doing in my medical practice. I called it self-hypnosis, and used it to teach my patients how to develop their inner resources to become self-confident in childbirth, or when facing surgery, chemotherapy, or the anxiety of phobias. In sports-related cases, the process helped golfers with problems like the putting yips or pre-tournament sleep disturbance.

When Rich Boswell, a top amateur golfer, had learned and become skilled in self-hypnosis to help control a medical problem, I suggested he also use those skills to improve his golf game. He created an image of the club-head going through the ball so it would do exactly what he wanted. By altering the image slightly, he could make the ball go high, low, draw or fade. That same year, play-ing with this imagery, he won a spot on the Provincial Amateur team. The last day of the tournament was played in the rain. He said that his new imagery helped him focus on his shot, not the rain.

The successful transfer of this life-skill to golf was the seed-idea for this program. When I asked prominent speakers at hypnosis conferences whether they had used hypnosis techniques for golf or other sports, they related experiences similar to mine. That is, each had responded to an athlete's problem as if he were a patient. Once the problem was solved, the athletes were encouraged to use self-hypnosis to enhance their imagery, and concentration skills to enhance performance.

● Training Your Inner Mental Skills

High-speed cameras, capable of "freeze-framing" minute aspects of the golf swing, have greatly improved our knowledge of swing mechanics. These have made teaching and learning the swing much easier. However, despite such technical advances, the average golf score has not changed appreciably. Nor have the average scores of tournament players, in spite of well-groomed courses and advances in equipment. Perhaps we haven't been giving enough attention to our Inner Mental Skills. One reason for this is the lack of ways and means to develop these Inner Mental Skills.

Over-analysis gets in the way of good shot-making. Golfers easily identify a distinct difference between a focused, seemingly effortless shot, and a shot suffering from "paralysis by analysis." Performance in sport involves a kind of "effortless effort." This requires concentration coupled with imagination, intuition, and active relaxation. (The term active relaxation means to have just the right balance between relaxation and a level of activation [arousal] essential for good performance.) The relaxation that golfers strive for in their shot-making is not the deep level found in techniques used for therapeutic ends. Rather, it is an active relaxation in which the muscles that oppose an active muscle have just the right amount of tone to allow that active muscle to function at its best. (See Chapter Two.)

Over a twenty-five year period, Dr. Lars Eric Unestähl, a Swedish sport psychologist, evolved mental training programs based on his research with athletes in all sports. He coined the term "Inner Mental Skills" to distinguish the concentration, relaxation, imagery, and intuition needed for performance. Most of these skills involve right brain activity. The logical, sequential analytical mental skills needed for problem solving are mainly Left Brain activity. They tend to be primarily focused on the world outside of ourselves. Inner Mental Skills enhance learning and aid in mastery of the golf swing. More important, they are the skills that help you perform well, to *play the game.*

Here, I would like to emphasize the word *training.* By this I mean that the skills are a part of everyone's make-up, that they *can* be learned and that the means to develop them *are* available. Although geared for golf, Inner Mental Training (IMT) principles apply to all sports, in fact to all performances. I have taught IMT principles to speed-skaters, to performers in the arts, to patients preparing themselves for surgery. The benefits of faster times, better form, more confidence in healing ability were very rewarding to the persons involved. Athletes who have taken this program tell me of the successful transfer of the skills to their everyday work lives, managing such things as the frustration of difficult meetings, or stress related to job interviews. Some have successfully used the skills to help manage medical problems like back pain, or have coped with stress and anxiety during acute illnesses.

Like all human capabilities, Inner Mental Skills vary from person to person. For most of us, the level of capability of our mental skills is somewhere near the average, just as for our golf skills. For some people, Inner Mental

Skills are an accepted part of their lives and the sports they play. Others, whose skills are less well-developed, may not make much use of these resources in their lives. This is often due to a lifelong habit of analyzing details coupled with a distrust of intuition, or simply a lack of knowledge about these mental skills. Moreover, in the education system we are taught to succeed with reasoning and analysis to solve problems. This learning focuses on a particular mental skill, logical sequential thinking, and depends largely on the spoken and written word. Conscious effort plays an important part in this mental skill. However, learning a new golf swing depends more on the "effortless effort" that is characteristic of Inner Mental Skills.

● How I Used Inner Mental Skills

I offer a personal anecdote to help illustrate the benefits of diligent practice of these skills. Three years ago a reader from Chicago, Bob Husmoller, sent me a brochure on Jack Kuykendall and his Natural Golf Corporation. Jack had developed a new swing theory and designed clubs to match the swing. He later met Moe Norman, the Canadian golf legend, whose swing matched the principles of the swing Natural Golf advocated. Moe, the most accurate ball striker in golf, had used this unorthodox swing for fifty years and thus validated the theory and the swing. Intrigued with their testimonials and theory, I bought a 6 iron and the teaching video. I was amazed at the accuracy and distance of my shots compared to my traditional swing and switched completely to Natural Golf clubs and swing. I learned a very different grip, stance and images for the swing. I attended a weekend school and the following year had a few hours of informal instruction from Todd Graves, a Natural Golf teaching professional who was then playing the Canadian tour. (See Golf Digest, December 1995, for an article on Moe Norman and a description of Natural Golf's swing theory.)

The change gave me an opportunity to put Mind-Body Golf's ideas into practice. I *committed* myself to trying this new swing for a full season. It was a radical change from a lifetime's use of the traditional swing and the images that went with it. In my altered state, I taught myself the images necessary for the changes and to assess and reassess the kinesthetic images as I progressed. When I hit a good shot, I paused to review images of the mental and physical parts of the swing I was working on.

How did I rate? My first year's scores were inconsistent, with one or two errors on several holes in most games. The second year, after learning about and doing the Progressive Relaxation Exercise (See Chapter Two) regularly, I became better at assessing the level of tension in different muscle groups. I became aware that when anxious, I habitually raised the tension in the muscles of my shoulders and chest. The solution to the problem came with time spent doing PMR, focusing particularly on these muscle groups, and using imagery to create a way to quickly relax these muscles.

In the second season I won my flight in the club championship and scored two aces, both during tournaments, the second during the club championship. My handicap is now lower than when I started the new swing. This season I achieved a lifelong goal, a one over par game, two strokes under my age.

When you commit time and effort to this program, you will find, like I did, that it positively

affects your view of yourself as a golfer. Your reward for the effort will be lower scores and more pleasurable golf. Using the skills in everyday living will be an added bonus.

Now turn on your CD player (or your computer's audio player) to listen to track 1, disc 1, the introduction to the exercises. Then take 15 minutes to do Exercise 1a on track 2. The theory will be explained more fully in the next chapter.

After doing the exercise, write about your experience. A sentence or two in a logbook will serve to record your reaction and ideas for future use. (See page 109 on writing notes in a diary.)

● Summary of Chapter One

Inner Mental Skills consist of concentration coupled with imagination, intuition, and active relaxation. They are the skills that help you perform well, to play the game. These skills are a part of everyone's makeup. Training improves them just as physical skills improve with training.

● Goals

- learn more about Inner Mental Skills to enhance learning and aid in mastery of your golf swing

- learn to manage emotions and negative thoughts and images of yourself that can produce poor performance

● Concrete application

Commit yourself to spending time and energy to train your Inner Mental Skills as you learn and groove your golf swing.

● Creative application

Think about the application of these ideas to your everyday life. Make a note of the ideas in your log-book for future reference.

Notes on chapter one

_____

_____

_____

_____

_____

_____

_____

_____

_____

_____

_____

_____

Chapter two

Relaxation for performance

● Active Relaxation

When too relaxed, you do not have the drive or the energy to play well. When too tense, mistakes follow from trying too hard. In no other sport is this more true than in golf. Most golfers have experienced the exhilaration of hitting a long ball

TEE TIPS

Keep your head down
Flex your knees
Firm up your grip
Loosen your grip
Watch the ball
Don't bend your elbow
Step into the ball
Don't rush your swing
Follow through
and

R E L A X

(Anonymous. From a poster on a clubhouse washroom wall.)

easily, with no apparent effort. Afterwards, they often remember being relaxed while making the shot. When they try hard to repeat that performance, the shot often goes awry. The reason is that when they try hard, they increase the tension in the muscles that oppose the muscles active in the swing. There is reliable scientific evidence which shows that lowering the tension in those muscles which oppose[1] muscles active in a complicated physical skill improves the performance of that skill.

Leif Janson, the Swedish national archery coach, used his electrical engineering knowledge to study muscle activity in archers as they shot arrows. He placed sensors over the muscles of his archers to measure electrical activity in the muscles as they made their shots. (This is called electromyography, or EMG for short. It is the indirect measuring of tension in the muscle located under a sensor.) Janson found that his best archers were expert at relaxing those muscles that opposed the muscles actively

---

1. When we perform an action, there is a muscle which is mainly responsible for that action. There is also a muscle whose main responsibility is to oppose that action with a monitoring force in order to make the primary action smooth. These are the opposing muscles for that action. For instance, a muscle like the triceps opposes the biceps in its attempts to bend the elbow, and the biceps opposes the triceps when it straightens the arm.

involved in the shot. In champions, these opposing muscles had just the right tone to make the action smooth. He found the same pattern in musicians who played stringed instruments. The best players were better at having the correct tone in their opposing muscles. Experience has shown him the importance of measuring the activity of opposing muscle groups. Having the right tone in these muscles is the essential component of Active Relaxation, and this is the platform on which the best performances occur. To study golfers, he took representative EMG tracings from the opposing muscle in the forearms of golfers in actual practice conditions, minimizing restriction by wires and sensors during the swing.

Janson made electromyographic tracings of the swings of several tour players at the Swedish Masters golf tournament in July, 1994. He reported his findings at the World Congress on Mental Training and Excellence, held in Ottawa in May, 1995. He measured the activity of muscles during each of ten shots by each player studied. The better players had smooth tracings in each shot, indicating that the opposing muscles did their job well and with no wasted effort. There was a remarkably constant level of tension at the start of each swing and when the ball was struck. However, the tracings of the less skilled players were much less smooth, indicating unnecessary muscle activity. This was true at the start of the shot and continued throughout the swing. The level of tension varied with each shot and at all stages of each swing. Janson also found that good golfers were so used to their own technique that they could not feel, or did not know, the muscle dynamics of their swing. Janson was able to teach these golfers to relax these muscles and this resulted in better performance.[2] (Illustrative tracings of the muscle activity in the swings of a touring professional golfer compared to that of a less-skilled golfer can be found in Appendix Two, page 124, Figures 5 and 5a. A more detailed description of this study is found there as well.)

---

2. The researchers wondered if these findings could be generalized to other learning situations. Speaking a new language involves new movements of the tongue and facial muscles as well as mastering a new vocabulary, so the researchers chose to study immigrants learning Swedish as a second language. They wished to determine whether learning would be enhanced if PMR exercises were done before the language classes began. They had one group of students do the PMR exercise emphasizing the tongue and facial muscles, while the second group learned the language without this preparation. The PMR trained group learned their new language faster and better than the group taught without this preparation.

● Relaxation and Learning

Learning any new complex muscle skill is helped by first learning how to relax the appropriate muscles. This is most true for adult learning. Use the relaxation exercise as a preparation when:

- learning your swing
- perfecting your swing

These studies also report that on average, most adults carry a level of tension in their muscles higher than is ideal for learning a new skill. Apparently it takes at least four weeks for an adult to learn the different feeling of tense muscles versus relaxed muscles. It also takes this length of time to learn how to control the relaxation level in particular muscle groups. Children who have not yet been subject to the stresses of modern living require much less time to learn this skill.

● Progressive Muscle Relaxation Exercise (PMR)

Dr. Edmund Jacobsen (1929) reported on Progressive Muscle Relaxation (PMR) as a means to successfully lower high blood pressure. The exercise remains one of the best of many methods to learn muscle relaxation. PMR is now a mainstay technique to teach general relaxation in stress reduction clinics.

In PMR you tighten each major muscle group, then relax and focus on the feeling of relaxation in those muscles for ten seconds or so. When a muscle is first tightened and then relaxed, there is a deeper sense of relaxation in that muscle than if you had simply tried to relax it. In PMR, muscle groups are tightened and then relaxed in sequence from the feet up, or the opposite, from head to toes. After one or two circuits of your body, a sense of overall relaxation develops. What is most important, in the context of this program, is learning the feeling of relaxation in those specific muscle groups used in the golf swing.

Uneståhl and his colleagues teach this exercise to athletes as a basic mental exercise. While biofeedback instruments are better for teaching how to relax a certain muscle, PMR costs nothing, is available at all times, and is effective. (Conference on Mental Training and Excellence, Ottawa, May 1995.) Leif Janson reports that the muscles farthest away from a person's center of gravity give the most information about that person's general tension level. This suggests that you should be sure to include the muscles of the hands, feet, and the muscles of your face when doing this exercise for golf. Foremost, however, pay attention to the muscles of the dominant forearm that are used for the uncocking action in the swing. Focus particularly on the muscles at the top of the forearm as these are the opposing muscles in this action. Having the correct level of relaxation in this muscle group is the essence of Active Relaxation for the golf swing and will result in an uncocking action that is smooth and powerful.

Exercise 1 is a PMR exercise geared to golf. The first run-through sequence on track 2 is meant for learning, and the explanations of how to tighten particular muscle groups add to the time. The second run-through on track 3 has briefer directions and emphasizes those muscles involved in the golf swing. This exercise (1b) is meant for practicing. Eventually, you will know the exercise by heart and will no longer need my words. Each time you finish this exercise survey your whole body to determine if any muscles are still too tense.

Having read thus far, you might stop and do Exercise 1a again while these ideas are fresh in your mind.

● Relaxation by Other Methods

Most techniques, such as biofeedback, self-hypnosis, guided imagery, visualization, etc., ask the person to relax as the process begins. When you relax, your mind becomes tranquil. You are less critical of ideas and suggestions when your brain is quiet. Brain electrical activity slows and moves more to the right hemisphere, the half of our brain more often involved in imagery.

Herbert Benson, a Harvard University cardiologist, studied practitioners of Transcendental Meditation (TM) who told him of the relaxed feeling they enjoyed while meditating. Not only did their voluntary muscles relax, there was a general slowing of metabolism. Their heart rate decreased, blood pressure dropped and breathing rate slowed, as did their brain waves. He coined the term "relaxation response" to indicate what was happening in the meditative state. He developed the theory that this is a natural physiological response, the opposite to the fight or flight response. (See page 75 for a description of this latter reflex.)

Dr. Benson examined other methods of developing a relaxed state. He found that there were common characteristics in all of the techniques:

- Sit comfortably

- Close your eyes to help empty your mind

- Allow your muscles to relax

- Breathe in quietly through your nose

- Allow the breath to go without force by relaxing your chest muscles

- Repeat a humming word like 'one' or 'OM' on breathing out

- Give yourself a definite time for the exercise, e.g., 10 minutes (TM practitioners say 20 minutes)

When you experience the relaxation response, not every muscle is completely relaxed as in deep sleep. When in hypnosis or the meditative state, you are usually sitting and therefore the muscles required to maintain this posture are working at the correct level of tension. However, the feeling generated is one of overall relaxation, and this is the feeling you will have after the PMR exercise.

● Combining Imagery and Relaxation

Relaxation is not easily achieved by an act of will. The harder you try to achieve it, the more elusive it seems. You can more easily relax with your other system of control, the use of imagery. This method will be elaborated on in the next chapter, but to show the power of relaxation and imagery, try the following exercise.

Choose a partner of about equal strength and height, face one another, and do the following:

Partner One

Place hands "palm up" on your partner's shoulders. Consciously tense all of your arm muscles to the maximum, even making fists to accentuate the stiffness.

Partner Two

Try to bend Partner One's arms at the elbow using a steady force. Do not jerk suddenly as you may injure.

Each partner judges the amount of force

needed to bend his arms, or conversely, to keep his arms straight.

Repeat the test with the following changes:

Partner One

Again, place your hands, palms up, on your friend's shoulders. This time, take a few moments to relax your arms and hands, then form an image of unbendable steel bars running through your arms from your shoulders, through your fingers and beyond. When this mental image is firmly established, signal your readiness.

Partner Two

Again, try to bend Partner One's arms at the elbow with a steady force.

● Result

Both partners may be surprised at Partner One's increased ability to keep his arms straight the second time around. Switching roles and repeating the process will show Partner Two the power of combining imagery with relaxation.

When developing your imagery for golf, focus on the feeling images in your kinesthetic sense. (Kinesthesia refers to your sense of position, movement and muscle tension.) Build on the active relaxation of important muscle groups using the PMR exercise. That is, only those muscles needed for the shot will need to be active. The opposing muscles will have just enough activity to make the movement smooth. All other muscles will have only the tone needed for a relaxed, comfortable athletic posture. This image of active relaxation will help you perform to your maximum efficiency, whether for a delicate chip shot, or for a long tee shot.

There must be a certain amount of activation, of competitiveness, of wanting to make a good shot. It is the balance of relaxation versus activation that is the goal of all athletic performance. Active relaxation is as important for the beginner as for the competent golfer.

● Summary of Chapter Two

A golfer who is too tense will play poorly. A golfer who is too relaxed will also play poorly. Golfers must know the feeling of a correct balance between the arousal needed to play and the relaxation necessary to perform well. The aim is to achieve this active relaxation, to recognize when you are in this state, and to know how to fine-tune the state.

● Goals

- to commit to a 30 day program of daily practice of PMR for golf

- to become increasingly aware of the feeling of relaxation in your main muscle groups

- to learn the correct level of active relaxation in those muscles important in the golf swing, particularly in your forearms and shoulders

- to focus on those muscles whose main task is to oppose the muscles active in the swing, because it is these muscles that give smoothness to your swing

● Concrete Application

Develop a quick survey of the muscle tone of the shoulders, arms, and grip muscles. Time the survey to one or two out breaths. Aim at the desired level of active relaxation.

● Creative Application

Assess the tone of your neck, chest, and shoulder muscles before, and then after, a stressful event, such as a presentation to a group or a job interview. Prepare yourself for a similar event in the future by practicing PMR, paying particular attention to those muscles.

Chapter three

Creating imagery for golf

"The world should o' followed the lead of Pith-uh-gor'-us."... "And 'tis this—*to ken the world from the inside*, not the outside as we've done. Like I showed ye wi' yer gowf shots there."

Shivas Irons

● Daydreaming Creatively

While watching a tournament on television in 1967, I was startled by one scene. A player was putting, and as he went through his preparation routine it began to rain heavily. By the time the ball rolled into the hole there was a significant amount of water on the green. To watch him, however, it was as if the sun were shining. He seemed unaware of any discomfort.

His behavior reminded me very much of that of

mothers whom I had taught to use self-hypnosis during childbirth. They learned to be so involved in an image that they seemed unaware of discomfort. I became intrigued and began to think of ways to try to duplicate that level of concentration in golf.

I noticed that when I putted well, I had a five part routine approach to the putt that seemed to make the stroke automatic. I formalized the routine to make sure that I checked each point. Now, when I walk onto the green, I check the slope and contour, the firmness of the ground, the grain and the length of the grass, the length of the putt, and finally I choose the line and weight. Then I place all that information into my mind trusting that it will come out correctly. I focus on the imaginary line the putter must pass over as it goes through the ball. I then use a simple hypnosis trick. I breathe in as the putter goes back and out as I stroke the putt. This triggers an automatic and trusted stroke.

Self-hypnosis and all similar practices (Yoga, Zen, meditation, deep relaxation, biofeedback, etc.) aim for the same neuro-physiological state. This is a mental state in which we function much like in a daydream. The person narrows awareness onto images in one of the senses:

seeing, hearing, feeling, or rarely, the sense of smell. There is usually a calmness of mind and a feeling of relaxation and of detachment from surroundings. This is a natural phenomenon, for we all daydream. When we daydream, our right brain is active and our usual dominant left brain becomes quiet, just as in meditation or hypnosis.

● Creative Images

In the 1947 movie, *The Secret Life of Walter Mitty*, Danny Kaye played a timid bank clerk. He was a meek clerk one moment, then the next, a famous Spitfire ace in the middle of an air battle. To Walter, everyday life and his dream life were equally real. He had a vivid imagination and fabulous daydreams. Daydreaming is an altered state. Self-hypnosis is a similar altered state over which we exercise control over our images.

One young boy with cancer used the altered state to manage uncomfortable treatment procedures and to mobilize his immune system. He described self-hypnosis as "being like daydreaming, only I control the dreams" (Dr. Karen Olness, Conference on Hypnosis in Children, Edmonton, 1989.) In self-hypnosis we direct our daydreams using suggestions that create images. When you or I create our own golf images they will be much closer to reality, unlike the fantasies of Walter Mitty.

Exercise 2 is an imaging exercise. We begin the exercise by using a shortened PMR routine. Then, I describe a garden scene to teach the creation of a relaxing image. In the scene I suggest images in each of your senses, sight, hearing, movement, and the sense of smell, to maintain and deepen the altered state. In the process, the images in one of your senses will be sharper and easier to achieve. This is a normal variation, as we all have a favorite sense system. I believe, however, that on some days this changes, and one sense system can be easier to access than the favored one, so it is best to practice with each of the senses when creating images for golf.

The negative visual image of a shot going astray may interfere with the positive image of a ball flying to the target. Counter these visual images with a kinesthetic image of the feel of the swing, or the sound of the ball being hit on the sweet spot of the club as you focus on meeting the ball with a square club-face. The first visual image recedes into the background as you make the shot.

● Images are Reality

Negative images often interfere in the real world and seem to outweigh the positive images you try to achieve. This is due to the emotions attached to images. For example, being angry with yourself for making a bad shot means that self-anger is the dominant emotion governing your next shot. This bond of emotion to the image of the shot you are about to make causes you unconsciously to expect a bad shot. Such recurring patterns can be broken using creative imagery.

Have you ever told yourself, "I had better not hit out of bounds," only to do just that? The only image created by this thought is of going out of bounds. The phrase "I had better not" is merely words and does not evoke an image. When we face a choice between what we would like to have happen and what our imagination perceives is about to happen, imagination wins every time. The image of the ball flying out of bounds wins out over the thought of what we want to happen.

Another way of thinking about this is that images are reality in our minds. The image of going out of bounds is like practicing that very shot, rather than the shot you really want to make. This reality of imaging was shown by an experimenter who attached sensors over the muscles of a downhill skier to measure the activity in his muscles. The skier used his self-hypnotic state to recall the image of himself racing on a specific course in great detail. The tracings demonstrated that not only were his muscles active, but the degree and scope of muscle activity followed the difficulty of the race course on that hill. His muscles were not as active as in an actual race, but active nevertheless. As far as the athlete was concerned, he was racing.

● Suggestion and Imagery

Once you focus on one sensation, it is very easy to slip into a dreamlike state. In such a relaxed state, self-suggestions are considered less critically, particularly if they are phrased in terms that evoke images. Perhaps this is because memories are often in images rather than in words: they appear complete, with feelings attached, like dreams.

In the recorded exercises, suggestions are in words that evoke images, an important distinction to make when creating suggestions for yourself. The suggestions often emphasize control of body systems. One example involves relaxing those muscles not directly involved in the action. These suggestions are then linked to the idea that the muscles of the walls of the internal organs become relaxed and are working quietly. Just like the voluntary muscles, these involuntary muscles also need the right tone to be at maximum efficiency for their work.

When you have learned to relax the muscles that make up the walls of blood vessels and the heart, you can modify your heart rate. You can learn to decrease digestive symptoms associated with high levels of anxiety. As you learn to control some of the symptoms of anxiety, the anxiety itself becomes manageable.

The distinguishing feature of hypnosis, over other similar disciplines, is that of suggestion. Each suggestion must pass the scrutiny of our intuitive sense if it is to be accepted. Intuition is based on a lifetime of experience. A suggestion made by another must fit our moral and intellectual self. This exercise (No. 2) is a model for self-hypnosis. I act as your hypnotist, guiding and teaching as I lead you through the experience. Eventually you will easily lead yourself through the experience. When I recently asked a patient about a cassette tape I made for her in my office, she said she no longer used the tape, that she knew the routine by heart and now uses her own words instead of mine. *All hypnosis is self-hypnosis.*

Human abilities vary from person to person. Many people have discovered self-hypnosis on their own. When they experience or read about these ideas, they often realize that they already use the skills to focus, to relax, or to create images necessary for their sport. However, most of us will have to work at learning the skills, just like learning the golf swing. This effort is worthwhile because these skills are also useful in everyday life.

One of the first suggestions made when you are led through the hypnosis experience is that your muscles will relax. This is why the Progressive Muscle Relaxation exercise is often used to begin the process of a hypnotherapy session, particularly with patients who are very anxious. Relaxation is then linked to breathing. When breathing out quietly without force, the diaphragm and the chestwall muscles are relaxed. Your elastic lungs then push the air out, a natural association with being relaxed as you focus on relaxed breathing. When you focus on one sensation, in this case your breathing, it is easier to develop a tranquil mind, to slip into an absorbed daydream-like state.

To the observer, the person in hypnosis may appear to be dozing. However, even though the person's eyes are closed and he seems unaware of his surroundings, the electroencephalogram (EEG) is that of an active awake brain. For the person experiencing the altered state of hypnosis, it is the opposite of sleep. He is actively focused on the image, thought, activity, or sensation with which he is involved. He is aware of his surroundings, but detached from them, unless they have a bearing on his task. And, like the woman using self-hypnosis while working hard in labour, the person need not even look asleep. A more familiar sport example is that of an athlete who is so involved in the game that she plays on with an injury, the pain of which would ordinarily immobilize her.

● Important Concepts in Exercise 2

Three ideas introduced in this exercise merit further explanation. These are:

Anchoring. It is a simple idea. You associate some one

thing in one of the senses (a movement, touch, sound heard, or something seen) with the feelings associated with a memory. A common experience is associating a song with feelings of love for another. Incidentally, a person with a phobia attaches certain associations to negative feelings, e.g., a person with a phobia to flying associates the sight of an airplane to fright. Anchoring works at the unconscious level even though the anchor itself can be a conscious act.

Inner Strength, Or Inner Coach. There is a part of ourselves that knows our strengths. This is the part that has seen us through many difficulties in the past. Think of it as a coach, helping us to develop our natural abilities. Being able to talk to and trust this inner voice can be extremely useful in handling golf problems. John Miller dealt with this in an article about his successes in the 1970s where he described it as listening to the "little voice[1] that talks to me." (Golf Illustrated, October 1990.) The most important reason for introducing this idea is to inject a dose of reality into your daydreams. Your inner coach will tell you whether your golf imagery is nearer to reality than fantasy.

1. Intuition is sometimes described as an "inner voice."

An Inner Mental Room. In your imagination you create a room with specific items which are used in the exercises. This room becomes your own private mental training workplace. This strategy will help you to isolate a mental practice place where you can focus your mental exercises on golf. For example, in the problem solving exercises, you create scenes and graphics on the imaginary television monitor in this room. The image of being in your inner mental room is also a confirmation that you are deeply enough into your altered state for the exercises to be effective.

This is a good place to put down the book and listen and do Exercise 2. The important concepts will be fresh in your mind at this point in your reading.

● Combine Relaxation and Imagery When You Golf

Assuming that you have now done the first two exercises in tandem with reading this book, let me illustrate creative imagery. Having experienced relaxation and imagery, combine the two in practice and while playing. Both methods can be done quickly and unobtrusively as you walk up to your ball just before you make your shot. Try them out first on the practice tee. Notice that as you become more practiced in this imagery, you become more focused on the shot.

- My trigger to start the automatic concentration process is the first step I take as I approach the ball. (Have you noticed that most tour players take five steps to reach the ball and take their stance?)

- As you stand behind the ball looking at your target, develop the image of a wave of active relaxation starting at the top of your head and flowing down your face, neck, shoulders, chest, and into your arms and hands and on down. Then move up to the ball, take your stance, and make your shot while this feeling is with you.

- A second way is to create an image of yourself playing with the ideal active relaxation you strive for. This feeling image could come from a memory of a best performance. Then imagine yourself moving into that image, becoming one with the image.

Your imagination is limitless for creating images, sometimes the more whimsical the better. My friend Philip adds this image: he imagines a large magnet which draws him into the latter image.

Notes on chapter three

● Summary of Chapter Three

Mental images are reality to our mind and body. When we have an image in our mind of the shot we are about to make, the neuro-muscular pathways are active for that shot. It is as if we had practiced the shot just before making the actual shot.

● Goals

- to commit to using imagery to enhance learning and to groove your golf swing

- to extend the use of imagery to playing conditions. Learn to focus on the image of what you wish to achieve, the ball landing on the target

- to practice imagery in all your sense systems, feeling the swing you are about to make or hearing the ball hit the sweet spot

- to practice focusing on the positive images of the shot you are about to make

● Concrete Application

When faced with a shot never played before, use imagery in more than one sense system to create the best possible shot in your mind, then focus on this image as you make the shot.

● Creative Application

Imagine yourself achieving the goal of having a very successful interview. Practice this imaging during the few days before the scheduled interview and while waiting to be called into the interview room.

Notes on chapter three

_____

_____

_____

_____

_____

_____

_____

_____

_____

_____

_____

_____

_____

_____

_____

_____

_____

_____

_____

_____

_____

Chapter four

Keeping your eye on the ball

"The ability to control thought processes, to concentrate on a task (e.g., to 'keep your eye on the ball') is almost universally recognized as the most important key to effective performance in sport."

Robert M. Nideffer

● Concentration

When you resolutely direct your attention toward one activity, either real or imaginary, other sensations are muted, even ignored. Narrowing your attention to a very few things is also one entry into the altered state of awareness, the hypnotic, or meditative state. This is similar to allowing yourself to become involved in an ordinary daydream. It is also an example of the effortless flowing concentration needed for good shot-making.

In team sports concentration involves limiting your reaction to important cues that come from a wide area of attention. This skill is called "soft eyes" by hockey players, and Wayne Gretzky is its acknowledged master. Concentration in golf involves the focus onto a narrow, restricted area of attention.

Concentration cannot be forced, it has to be effortless. As you are about to make a shot, suddenly thinking "I must concentrate," may cause your concentration to disappear. Trying hard to concentrate is sure to fail, because concentration and voluntary effort do not go together. Jack Nicklaus looks intensely focused during every shot. Jack has said that playing the ball to a target in a certain way depends 10 percent on his swing, 40 percent on his setup and stance, and 50 percent on his mental picture. To achieve concentration, he becomes absorbed in his imagery. He says, "First I see the ball land in the target area, then the flight of the ball to that target, and finally, I focus on the feeling of the swing for that shot." Remember that images are reality to our minds. Jack's method is like practicing the shot just before he makes it. Like the skier described in Chapter Three, his muscles are busy with the image of the swing.

Try this method the next time you practice. As you stand behind the ball, pick a target within reach of an easy short iron shot. Actively image the flight of the ball to the landing target and then rolling up to the actual target. As you move up to the ball and take your stance, imagine the feel of the swing for that shot. Make the shot with only this image in your mind. Develop the practice of stopping for a moment or two after each shot to reassess the imagery. You might find a key part of the imagery which can become the trigger move to make the shot happen automatically. Practice hitting different shots like imagining you have to hit out of trees. When you have to play these shots in a game, you will find yourself thinking positively and much better able to focus on what you want to achieve.

Practice like this makes you more proficient in your imaging capability and improves concentration on the shot facing you. You learn to depend less on your analytical *what if* thinking and to rely more on the images of the shot you are about to make. Practice imaging during quiet times in your day. Include conditions of actual play in your images and you will improve the capacity to refocus quickly in the face of distraction.

● Anchors and Anchoring

Golfers are often frustrated when they try to transfer their fine practice fairway shots to playing the golf course. Many excellent magazine articles have outlined good practice routines. All stress two things. First, be wary of routinely hitting one ball after another, and second, practice with a purpose in mind. I would add a third. Practice your mental game each time you are on the practice fairway or green, even for your warm-up session before a game. Pause to review the image of good shots, perhaps even closing your eyes to do so. This is important if you are working on one aspect of the swing. Make sure you repeat your pre-shot routine, if not each time at least every third shot or so, even if it is only in your mind because of physical limitations of the practice area.

Here is a way to enhance moving your good practice shots to actual play. You learned the idea of anchoring in Exercise 2, where movement and touch were associated with the feelings of confidence, relaxation and control in the image that you were involved with. When good shots follow one another, create an anchor to fix the feelings of confidence, of active relaxation and trust in yourself that are a part of good shot-making. Spend time focusing on the tempo of your good shots and create an anchor for this feeling. My friend Rich takes out his favourite club (the feel of this club is his anchor) and swings it through the long grass beside the tee to reinforce or regain his feel for his best tempo.

Remember your other sense systems. Pay attention to the sound of the ball being struck on the sweet spot. Look for a visual anchor, like the position of the clubhead behind the ball. Anchors work at the subconscious level although the anchor itself is a conscious act. In other words, you do not have to think about what the anchor will do. Just do it.

● Memories Can Be Anchored

Another way to create an anchor is to recall an image of a time when you played a particular part of your game very well. I used this anchoring method with Darryl James during a tournament after he told me that he had developed a fear of greenside sand shots. He said he was lucky to be leading the tournament even though I had seen him make a great shot out of a fairway bunker to within five feet of the pin.

After this round, we spent time in the practice sand trap. I asked him to close his eyes for a moment, to access his memory bank to recall a time when he felt completely confident playing these shots. He easily remembered making small bets on holing out shots from the sand when he was a teenager, and winning most of the money. With this imagery in his mind, he began to hit excellent shots. Then I asked him to find one particular constant thing in one of his sense systems and to play several shots with this single image in mind. We allowed a rest time before changing to the next system. He was able to find a constant in each system, but the most powerful was an action in his kinesthetic system. This was the positioning of his right hand on the club just so, his last move before making the shot.

He continued to practice this anchor until he was sure it worked. He was also to practice the anchor in his imagination when he was not playing and to reinforce it while practicing sand shots. On the 17th hole of the last round his tee shot ended in the trap. He now faced a 50 foot shot to a pin set close to the far greenside with a sharp drop-off into a large pond. He made a magnificent shot to about 3 feet, and went on to win the Provincial Amateur title by one stroke.

● An Anchoring Exercise

Let's use chipping as our example, since we all have days in which every chip is good. Let's assume that your chipping game has deteriorated so that you have become anxious when you face any chip. This is how you structure a practice chipping session:

- Spend a few moments getting the memory of good chips into your mind. Take the time to fill in as much detail as possible.

- Fix the image by anchoring it in one of the senses. This might be hearing the clubhead hit the ball, looking at a spot on the ball, or placing a finger a certain way on the grip. Only your imagination limits the scope of examples. Do take some time with this part of the exercise.

- Practice using that anchor until satisfied that it is fixed in your subconscious. This will then become the anchor you use when, in a tense situation, you feel anxiety rising.

- Practice using the anchor in your image mode during quiet times in your day. When you become aware of your Ultradian Rhythm you can identify your "take a break" periods to do this. (Appendix Two expands on the phenomena of Ultradian Rhythms.)

The problem-solving techniques outlined here and those learned on Exercises 8 and 9, can be extremely useful even though the simulated problems are not the most pressing problems for you. When you practice the simulations on the CD, you gain a framework to solve your own unique problems.

● Triggers

Repetition increases concentration. This is why pre-shot routines are so effective an aid for concentration in sport. Repetitive activity is often used to help induce the altered state, like the movements in Tai-Chi or the repetition of the mantra in TM. In the recorded meditation exercises, I use the same ritual each time I lead you into a new exercise. In this way, I capture your attention and then maintain your focus as I describe images of what we wish to accomplish. In golf, you must develop a consistent approach to each shot. Use the same movements in the same order to move yourself into a focused mode, to help make your shot-making a smooth automatic event. The word **trigger** in the context of mental skills refers to the use of an action to begin an automatic activity. There are many intricate activities in everyday life that we have learned to do easily. All start with a movement or action which moves us into an automatic mode, the mind's way of conserving energy instead of having to think about every step of the action. With repetition a trigger becomes a useful tool to make shot-making an automatic process. It should be the first action in your pre-shot routine. Tour player Lee Janzen's aiming along his club at the target as he begins his final walk to his setup to the ball is a dramatic example of a trigger in golf.

Develop triggers to begin moving yourself into the automatic mode of shot-making, where everything happens smoothly. Make the trigger an action like Lee Janzen's, or the time-honoured forward press, to make your swing an automatic experience. The best triggers are ones you design for yourself on the practice tee.

● Negative Triggers

A movement which has become part of a routine can become fixed in your unconscious as a **negative trigger**[1]. If you have developed a change for the worse in your shot-making, use self-hypnosis to review in detail your pre-shot routine. Use the monitor in your mental room to watch yourself perform. Allow yourself to become involved in details to deepen your altered state and to search for a new move that has crept into your swing. Place this movie in your memory bank and then recall a time when you were making good shots consistently and review these shots in detail. Compare the two swings and you may find that a different move has become a negative trigger and is the reason for the change. This technique sounds complicated, but remember when you are in your image mode it is quick and simple. It has been an effective means to end goal scoring slumps in professional hockey players.

In 1995, I reviewed my routine to find out why there was such a difference between practice and play in my game. In practice I made shots with a smooth transition

---

1. Researchers studying musicians found such a negative trigger in a wind instrument player. It was the act of gripping the instrument as she began her performance. The trigger was so powerful that the increased tension persisted even with relaxation training. Eventually she had to suspend performing for a time until the trigger lost its effect and she learned a new trigger for her routine to begin the performance on a positive note.

to the downswing. However, during a game this smoothness often changed. I grabbed the club at the top of my backswing and tensed the muscles of my upper body as I did so. I made a grunting sound as I did this. However, I learned that if I had no air in my chest I could not grunt and was more likely to remain relaxed through this part of my swing. I am gradually challenging this habit by following a common practice of baseball pitchers in their pre-pitch routine, in which they breathe deeply and blow all the air out just before they throw the ball. A smaller breath out just before the club goes back is the last conscious act in my pre-shot routine and is helping me attain a smoother swing.

Triggers are like anchors in that they also work at the unconscious level. However, an anchor is a conscious act that recalls positive feelings associated with a previous event. While a trigger helps to make an action an automatic event, an anchor is something held in reserve to be used when negative feelings are interfering with your play.

● Summary of Chapter Four

Concentration is essential for good shot-making. Anchors and triggers are easily learned, and practical strategies to improving concentration on the shot you are about to make.

● Goals

- find and practice anchors that will override negative feelings when faced with a shot in tense situations
- develop a trigger to start your pre-shot routine to move your shot-making into automatic mode
- allow yourself to become involved with the images of what you wish to accomplish in the shot facing you

● Concrete Application

Use the anchor learned in Exercise 2 to reinforce the feelings of relaxed confidence the next time you face a shot that you often mess up in a tense situation.

● Creative Application

Use this same anchor next time you are faced with a situation outside of golf. Then find and develop other anchors that you can use in different situations, anchoring to different positive feelings.

Notes on chapter four

_____

_____

_____

_____

_____

_____

_____

_____

_____

_____

_____

_____

_____

Notes on chapter four

Chapter five

Playing golf with a positive mental attitude

"A bad shot was never on my mind. Every time I got over the ball I wondered how good the shot was going to be. I knew it was going to be good. But how good?"

Moe Norman (from Moe's Musings,
by Lorne Rubenstein)

● Habitual Negative Self-talk

How often does one hear golfers say "I can't putt worth a damn," or make other negative comments about their game? The way many golfers put themselves down after a bad shot may be a harkening back to family adages learned in childhood, because in our culture we frequently say things in a negative way to reinforce a point. The problem with this kind of talk is that we learn to accept a negative suggestion too easily.

Negative reactions often have powerful emotions attached to them. Even a minor error can key into these emotions which can then simmer for several holes and overpower the positive images that can get you back on track. One of my original students said, "If I get angry after a bad putt, I don't recover for five holes."

It is difficult by an act of will to turn negative emotions into positive ones, because such feelings are involuntary responses. They can be willed out of awareness, but they remain in the subconscious as negative images, often with strong emotions attached to them. They may emerge at inopportune times in varying degrees of severity. The real problem with this negative self-talk (becoming angry at yourself, or putting yourself down) is that it increases the likelihood of the bad play repeating itself. Negative self-talk becomes a negative affirmation and you expect the bad shot to happen again.

● Dealing with Strong Negative Memories

Strong negative memories form during experiences of severe emotional and/or physical stress. They have powerful emotions attached to them, so they are often called "visceral memories." Hormones and other messenger molecules flood the body during these stressful events and cause the symptoms of the fight or flight response: the rapid pulse, trembling hands, dry mouth, and tight feeling in the stomach, etc. These substances are stored, ready for immediate use should a similar event occur. Even the memory of that event will trigger their release. When we remember an event we also recall and feel the associated feelings. This is because the hormones and other messenger molecules are triggered by that memory, or by a similar experience.

If the original stress situation created large amounts of these substances, there is an overabundance stored and ready for action. A minor event that is similar to the original can trigger the release of larger amounts of these substances, giving rise to stronger symptoms than the new situation warrants. For a person who becomes overly anxious when speaking in public, a less threatening situation, like being asked to speak in a small meeting, may release far more of these messenger molecules than is warranted. The level of anxiety is out of proportion to the situation. An excessive fear of speaking in front of a group of strangers is similar to having to play a shot in front of several strangers. For this person the similarity may be enough to release the stored hormones and induce symptoms out of proportion to the severity of the situation. Performance suffers. In this way the body can work against us at times. It is usually called an anxiety response and when the anxiety is overwhelming, becomes a phobic response.

How can you manage situations that trigger an anxiety response? One way is to first acknowledge the signal for what it is: a negative suggestion that the same feelings will occur in any similar situation. Then, make up an alternate positive thought or affirmation. Phrase it in the present tense, as if already achieved. Avoid negatives like "I am not anxious." Make up a positive phrase like "I am calm." In the meditative state, create a positive image of the behavior change you have in mind. Make up an affirmation, a word or phrase that evokes the image of achieving that goal. Repeat the affirmation often, without force, like a whisper in your mind, to reinforce your subconscious image. The negative thought or suggestion will gradually lose its force, or disappear. The affirmation, the image of the changed behavior, will then become a part of the way you view yourself as a golfer — your self-image.

● Affirmations for Golf

Throughout this program, I suggest that you practice the altered mode of control, the meditative state, and that this is the most efficient way to achieve behavior change. When your brain is quiet it approaches problems in a more intuitive, holistic, right brain way. The left brain, our dominant analytic mode of functioning, is in the background. Images are powerful. When a positive affirmation is used, it is the images recalled by the affirmation that will control the shot you are about to make.

Meditation exercises on the CD's describe the images I use when I want to be positive in golf, how I lead up to concentrating on reaching my target. I have chosen four C-words[1] that evoke images that help me to fix my thoughts on any golf shot: I am ... **Consistent, Committed, Confident, Concentrating**. For me, each word and the image it evokes is important for becoming and remaining focused on any golf shot. The ideas and images that these words represent to me are woven into meditations. (Exercises 3, 4, 5, and 6.)

---

1. Uneståhl collected the power words and phrases that top athletes developed for themselves. He found that most words began with the letter "C."

Creativity is another C-word worth further consideration. Darryl James, a former top amateur golfer now playing on the Canadian tour, creates the image of a crowd encouraging him in tournaments because he plays better with a friendly encouraging crowd following him. Images like these are easy to employ, and since they are unique to you, are very effective. Amy Alcott, the L.P.G.A. tour player, says that she thinks of each of her shots as a new Creation. In every round we may face one or two shots that we have never had to play before and more than our usual **Creativity** is required.

Here is another good break point in your reading. Get out disc 2 and do Exercise 3, the first meditation exercise. These 4 exercises are each about 8 minutes long. I find it best to do one, or at the most two of these exercises at one sitting.

● **Other C-Words**

Other words, also beginning with the letter C, may be more important to your game. Competent, Challenging, Courageous, Complete, and Childlike (my image of "Childlike" is that of a youngster playing games with abandonment and joy), are examples that could be made into affirmations for your game. Not all focus words in golf begin with the letter C, so a friend adds the C-word Capable to keep the idea of C-words going. He makes up affirmations for his golf, like "I am capable of finding and maintaining my best tempo." An example I have used effectively during a game is "I am capable of chipping this ball close."

Each meditation exercise stresses muscle relaxation because it is important in golf. I also emphasize the idea of control in each exercise. Your meditations, repeating the suggestion of being relaxed in a controlled way, will make this image part of your golf game. They will spill over into your everyday activities and ease job related stress.

● Wandering Thoughts

When meditating, your thoughts may wander. To counter this, there is a natural desire to get back on track, to follow the induction pattern again. However, this is analytical, left brain activity and is often counterproductive. It is best to allow the wandering thoughts to go on.

Don't fight them. Just allow the main thought to come back into your focus easily and naturally, helped by repeating the focus word. Simply allow yourself to be captured, to become absorbed in the images of the meditation.

If outside noises intrude, like music playing or people talking, change the way you process the noise. Rather than letting yourself become involved in the meaning of the words, focus on the qualities of the sounds and use these to deepen the meditation. Allow the rhythm of the music, or the cadence of the talking, to form the background to your imaging and continue to meditate in a passive, accepting way. Practice this a few times, then transfer the skill to the golf course. When noises or movements around you are processed in this way, your level of concentration on your shot will become more acute. To prepare for a tournament, practice for it by asking your partners to talk or move during your shots in casual rounds and you soon become expert at refocusing in the face of distraction.

Meditation, to be really useful to you, requires practice. Transcendental Meditation (TM) practitioners meditate for twenty minutes twice daily. Longer and more frequent sessions are a tradition in prayer rituals in monasteries of all religions. It is important to develop the habit of daily practice. Frequent shorter periods of daydreaming about golf, particularly when you *direct the dreams*, may be equally effective. For example, commit to two weeks of twice daily practice of making several 4 foot putts. Focus on the *feel* of your head being still until you *hear* the ball falling into the cup.

We all daydream just as we dream as part of our night-time sleep. Daydreams have a rhythm, an average cycle of 90 to 120 minutes like our nighttime dream cycles. The brain seems to require a rest from its usual analytical and logical mode of functioning and it refreshes itself by slipping into daytime reveries that last about twenty minutes. The brain also changes its control system and allows body organs to go into their resting mode. That is why a yawn and a stretch are often part and parcel of these reveries. EEG tracings show a definite shift to right brain dominance during these episodes. They are very much like meditative states and, in effect, you are half way into a meditation so a portion of the time could be used to reinforce your positive images in golf. (See Appendix Two for more information on Ultradian Rhythms.)

● Right Brain/Left Brain Theory

When we are in the meditative state (the altered mode of functioning), we treat ideas in a somewhat different way than we do when we are in our usual or dominant mode of functioning. In the altered mode, we rely more on intuition and we tend to view the whole idea, rather than analyze each part in sequence. This is what happens when you walk away from a problem that appears unsolvable, then come back later to solve it easily.

There is no really satisfactory explanation underlining the phenomena observed in these altered states. A current view is that the process is connected to our ability to switch between our two ways of processing information, from the dominant verbal mode to an image mode. Since the right side of the brain processes information in images and the left side in words, this fits the "left brain/right brain" theory of brain function. EEG studies tend to support this hypothesis, since the right, image-processing side of the brain is more active in the altered states of daydreaming, hypnosis, and meditation.

Figure 1: The contrasting functions attributed to Right/Left brain (After Uneståhl)

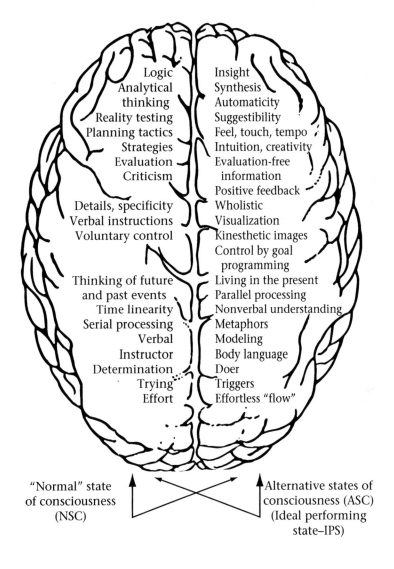

Logic
Analytical
thinking
Reality testing
Planning tactics
Strategies
Evaluation
Criticism

Insight
Synthesis
Automaticity
Suggestibility
Feel, touch, tempo
Intuition, creativity
Evaluation-free
information
Positive feedback

Details, specificity
Verbal instructions
Voluntary control

Wholistic
Visualization
Kinesthetic images
Control by goal
programming

Thinking of future
and past events
Time linearity
Serial processing
Verbal
Instructor
Determination
Trying
Effort

Living in the present
Parallel processing
Nonverbal understanding
Metaphors
Modeling
Body language
Doer
Triggers
Effortless "flow"

"Normal" state
of consciousness
(NSC)

Alternative states of
consciousness (ASC)
(Ideal performing
state–IPS)

There is evidence that during a peak performance the right brain is more active.

There has been considerable research into split brain theory and its application to many human endeavors, from creativity to all types of performance. Many different functions have been assigned to either side. You can think of the differences in simple terms. The left side of the brain is analytical and logical, it processes information sequentially in units, and it uses words as its mode of expression. The right brain is spatial and intuitive, it processes information simultaneously and holistically (a word that has come to mean the putting together all parts of an idea, or a problem, into one package), and uses images as its mode of expression.

Test this idea by describing in words a golf swing that you have just made. Then do the same using images of what you felt, saw and heard while making the swing. I think you will find that the latter is easier to do. This contrast may be one reason why it is difficult to teach and to learn a physical skill like the golf swing. The learner has a more important part to play in the process than does the teacher, because the learner has to translate a wordy description of a skill into her own images and sensations. However, we also need to know facts and principles to understand the golf swing. The best human performances occur when the functions of each side of the brain are integrated and synchronized.

To make the process more useful consider how you make a shot in the context of right/left brain function. The left brain activity begins by considering the target, the weather, the hazards. Then you plan the shot, select the club, step up to the ball, and take your stance in relation to the target. At this point you shift to right brain activity: you visualize the flight of the ball to the target, form a kinesthetic image feeling the movements of the stroke and then make the shot with this single narrow focus of attention.

I chose four model meditation exercises: Consistence, Committed, Confidence, and Concentration. These particular C-words are linked to positive outcomes. Meditating on these focus words will counter those negative thoughts that can get in the way of the golf you are capable of playing.

Summary of Chapter Five

It is important to understand the influence of self criticism, of negative self-talk, of giving ourselves negative expectations, like "I never make these three-foot putts." It is far more productive to think success rather than failure.

Goals

- transform negative self-talk into positive affirmations

- employ images while in your altered state. Saying the affirmation word (or words) will evoke these images

- repeat the affirmation to bring forth the expectation of a positive result like, "I can make these three-foot putts in all circumstances."

Concrete application

When faced with a difficult shot, combine affirmations. For example, "I am Confident. I look forward to the Challenge of this shot."

● Creative application

When faced with a stressful situation like a job interview, take a few moments to recall a less stressful situation. Savor the feeling of confidence you had when you expressed yourself easily and comfortably. Then employ an affirmation that evokes these feelings and say it quietly to yourself as you approach the interview. Practicing the technique for golf will reinforce the use of the skill in other life situations.

Notes on chapter five

_____

_____

_____

_____

_____

_____

_____

_____

_____

Notes on chapter five

Chapter six

Activation versus relaxation

"It's not a question of getting rid of butterflies, it's a question of getting them to fly in formation."

Jack Donohue

(Canadian Olympic Basketball Team Coach)

● Losing Active Relaxation

Have you ever stood on the tee with a good score going, but with three other foursomes ahead of you? You are ready to play, but forced to wait. You feel that you may lose your rhythm. You become bored and wonder if you can prepare for the tee shot before cooling down too much. You are too relaxed, so you need to psyche yourself, reactivate yourself to continue to play well.

Studies have repeatedly shown that best performances occur when the level of activation is a little below that level where anxiety develops. The relationship between activation and athletic performance is usually illustrated as an inverted U curve. That is, there is a positive relationship between increasing activation and performance up to a certain level of activation. Beyond that point, over-arousal develops into anxiety. When this occurs performance suffers, or breaks down entirely. It is very difficult to get back to the correct level of active relaxation without using one's Inner Mental Skills (see Figure 2.)

Figure 2

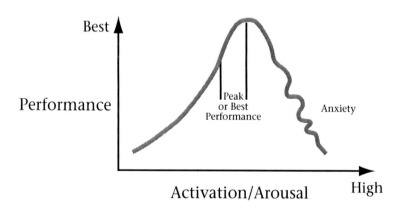

Figure 2: a stylized inverted U curve showing the relationship between activation/arousal and performance. The line becomes irregular when past the apex to indicate that it is difficult to move back once anxiety symptoms develop.

The curve in Figure 2 is true for all sports, in fact for all performances. For football linebackers or weightlifters, who require a high level of activation to explode into action, the curve starts more to the right on the arousal scale. The curve also explains why, even in these athletes, too much activation leads to poor performance. For sports like golf and archery, the curve starts closer to the left side of the arousal scale because these sports require less activation to perform well.

● Fight Or Flight Response

Activation mainly involves stimulating the sympathetic nervous system, resulting in the production of hormones like adrenaline, cortisone, and other agents. The effects are a faster heartbeat, deeper and more rapid breathing, a very active and alert mind, and an increase in strength and energy. Blood is diverted from the digestive system to the muscles and to the brain, to prepare for impending physical and mental activity. The heart pumps more blood with each beat, and blood pressure rises. This is the sympathetic stress response, or the fight or flight response. Athletes are aware of these symptoms and feelings. They call it being pumped up, or say, "The adrenaline was really flowing."

When these physiological changes are excessive, balance is lost and things become chaotic. The heart rate becomes too fast, the breathing irregular, and the muscles fail to work smoothly. Most of us are familiar with these symptoms, since most of us have been in situations that produce anxiety symptoms. For example, you may have experienced this standing on the first tee preparing to drive with several people watching. Your heart rate jumps, your mouth becomes dry, and your hands feel shaky and unsteady.

For people with phobias, these symptoms can reach alarming levels, and can deeply affect their ability to perform. (A phobia is an exaggerated fear reaction to a situation or object that most people accept as ordinary.) The common manifestation of a phobia in golf is the putting yips, which may become so severe that the putter blade feels frozen to the green, and the stroke becomes a jab. A golfer with this problem has many symptoms of a phobic reaction. Fortunately, since the putting yips is often a recently learned reaction, the person can re-learn the response and eliminate this overreaction using a combination of relaxation and imagery.

● Modifying Physiological Functions

In the past, physicians thought the fight or flight response was reflex and out of our control: a response to the need to survive. However, using the meditative state, you can learn to control the symptoms to strike just the right level of activation for the task facing you. You do this using the skills learned so far: to slow your heart rate, alter your breathing pattern, and lower the level of tension in your muscles. If you were a computer, you would be reprogramming the software in your brain. By controlling the symptoms of anxiety you control the level of the sympathetic stress response, the modern term for the fight or flight reflex.

Exercise 7 provides you with images to increase blood flow to your hands and fingers. These images are based on normal physiological activity controlled by the mind through the brain. Use a digital thermometer to test this on yourself. Hold the sensor tip of the thermometer in the web between two fingers and take a reading. (This reading may be below the lowest temperature on its scale. If this is true, pay attention to the location of the lower reading. The important thing here is to note the rise in temperature above the lowest reading.) Start exercise 7 and take another reading when finished the exercise. During this exercise, I provide suggestions and images to increase blood flow to your fingers. Your finger temperature will go up by a degree or more because of the increased blood flow to your fingers.

This is another break point to stop reading and get out disc 2. Do Exercise 7 while these ideas are fresh in your mind.

When the outside temperature drops, blood flow to the skin is reflexively reduced to preserve body heat. The purpose of this reflex is to preserve life in much more serious conditions than playing golf on a cool, rainy day. Learn to modify this "cold reflex" using your alternate mode of control: create suggestions and images that cause the walls of blood vessels supplying the skin to relax. This exercise example simulates the experience of playing in cold weather. The increased blood flow to the skin which results will modify the heat-preserving reflex because the temperature sensors of the body are in the skin. This is like raising the thermostat in your house to increase the output of the furnace.

You can also use your mental control system to provide the opposite effect, playing in very warm weather. For some people, perspiration in warm weather gets out of hand, as if their cooling reflex was an all-or-none phenomenon. Learn to control this reflex by creating images that make your sweat glands slow their production of sweat. Decrease the blood flow to the sweat glands by creating suggestions to increase the tone of the muscles of the walls of the arteries to the glands. The wisdom of the body will ensure that there is just enough sweat to evaporate and cool the body. Preserving your body water will be an added bonus!

Another common problem, unrelated to golf, is excess salivation while the dentist is working on your teeth. Use your mental skills, while waiting for the procedure, to develop the altered state and create the image of your mouth being dry, as if dehydrated. Reduced saliva means less swallowing and so less discomfort while the dentist works on your teeth.

Using your self-hypnosis skills like this can give you control over many unpleasant situations. Create and practice them in your imagination

**before you have to use them in real
life. In this way you are prepared
for the situation when it does
develop.**

Notes on chapter six

_____

_____

_____

_____

_____

_____

_____

_____

_____

_____

_____

_____

_____

Summary of Chapter Six

It is important to be able to activate yourself and to become aware of the feelings associated with the correct level of activation. Imagery and suggestions are used to establish the balance of activation and relaxation that is a part of a good performance.

Goals

- to tune in to your body's response to various situations
- to know when a muscle is properly prepared for action
- to know when its opposing muscle has the correct tone to make that action smooth and powerful
- to extend this control to other organ system activities

Concrete Application

Practice the energizing breathing imagery when losing energy or when fatigued while playing.

● Creative Applications

Become alert to situations in your life, like attending a meeting when tired and where it is important to psyche yourself up for an important event. Use the simple energizing breathing imagery to prepare for these events.

Notes on chapter six

Chapter seven

Setting goals to improve your golf

"Today's goals are tomorrow's realities."

Terry Orlick

● Setting and Reassessing Your Goals

Your interest in this program suggests you have a goal, even if it is just a general desire to satisfy your curiosity about Golf: The Mind-Body Connection. "What could Inner Mental Training do for me?" In every field of human activity, research into goal setting has reinforced what every outstanding athlete knows instinctively, that setting goals improves performance. Specifically:

- working toward a goal improves self-confidence and motivation. It also decreases performance anxiety

- performance goals, playing to personal standards set by yourself, are more effective than outcome goals, such as winning a tournament or match

- people who create images of themselves having achieved their goals are more likely to succeed in reaching them

Athletes need the motivation of wanting to win over an opponent. However, they soon learn that focusing on winning a competition is far less effective than concentrating on performing at their best. Ingemar Stenmark, the Swedish slalom ski-racer, worked out an ideal race for each hill. He was satisfied if he raced close to this ideal even if he did not win. His system worked — he won more than his share of races!

Goal setting begins with beoming aware of your present situation. Develop a picture, or write a description of where you are now, then develop a picture of the level of play you would like to achieve. You do not need a lofty goal. A worthwhile goal can be to play at a level good enough to play with friends, to enjoy the companionship and the recreation that golf provides. However, most golfers look forward to the self-satisfaction of improved shot-making, a best score, or a lower handicap.

Keep a diary of your games and your practice sessions. This is an excellent way to develop and assess performance goals. A diary will pinpoint the parts of your game that need improvement. It also tells you whether goals are being achieved and whether they need updating.

The details and a model diary are contained in Appendix One. The model uses an ordinary scorecard to make notes of your different shots as the game progresses. These notes become the data for a statistical record of your games. They also act as an *aide mémoire* for a narrative diary of your mental game. This model highlights the different parts of the game, providing you a way to assess your game and update your goals. Most important, the first statistic you work out is of the good shots in that game.

● Performance Goals

Setting goals does not appeal to everyone. To you, it might look like too much of a hassle, something that is overdone nowadays. Besides, how does one handle failing to achieve a goal? This is a very realistic question for many people. Dr. Terry Orlick says that self-acceptance is the most overlooked aspect in the process of setting goals. In his extensive experience with athletes, he has never met an athlete who intentionally messed up a performance. Therefore, your first goal should be to like yourself and recognize yourself as a good person, able to learn from every experience.

Make the very important distinction between a performance goal: playing to a standard that you set for yourself, as opposed to an outcome goal, "I am going to win my flight in the club championship this year." The problem with outcome goals is that you can control your own performance, but not the performance of others, nor a rub-of-the-green. Someone can have his career best round in that tournament.

Note: Performance goals can be divided roughly into short-term, intermediate-term, and long-term. The following are important things to remember when setting your performance goals:

Incorrect:

- make 20 out of 20 10-foot putts. Start over if you

> miss one putt, and don't leave the practice green
> until you have reached that goal

Even some tour players would have difficulty with that one! Fatigue, or a sore back, may cause mistakes. There is no point in trying to "work through them" by practicing those mistakes. It would be wiser to take time off from physical practice and use the meditative state to review images of your best putting games. When these are compared to your present practice, errors that have crept into your swing will often be exposed, the first step in correcting them. In fact, athletes with well-developed Inner Mental Skills use this technique (of reviewing their technical skills while in the altered state) to get out of a slump.

Correct:

- set a specific short-term goal in putting practice:

- make 10 of 10 putts from 12 to 18 inches

- . . . 9 of 10 from 2 feet

- . . . 7 of 10 from 3 feet

- . . . 6 of 10 putts from 5 feet (even the pros do not succeed in making 100 percent of putts from 5 feet!)

The breakdown of your game into its various parts, like this putting game example, is elaborated upon in Appendix One. Set similar practice standards for pitches and chips, a part of your short game. An intermediate goal could be to lower your short game scores. Both examples are short term-goals within this intermediate goal. Achieving successive goals like these improve your chances of accomplishing a longer term-goal, like a lower handicap within a certain time limit.

● Achievable Goals

Aim at performance goals that are specific and measurable like those suggested. Keep them simple. Begin with a few achievable goals rather than too many goals, too soon. This keeps goal setting in perspective and keeps you focused on progress. A goal must motivate, not rule your life. Reward yourself by setting short-term goals that are believable and achievable within a short time frame. You do want to boost your morale as you work toward a long term goal!

Goals must be an improvement over your present performance. Set them high enough to be challenging and realistic enough to be achievable. In Chapter One I talked about our inner coach, the part of ourselves that knows our strengths and weaknesses very well. Your inner coach can guide you and help to set and reassess your goals.

Write down long-term and intermediate goals. Express them in the present tense, in positive terms, and in words that create an image of yourself achieving the goal. Be wordy to start with, then rewrite your goals in progressively shorter forms, until stated in just a word or two. These become your power words, your affirmation phrases. Motivate yourself by assigning realistic target dates. Review the goals periodically to give yourself a reference point. Periodic reviews like this also reveal whether your goals are closer to reality than fantasy, or whether they need to be revised to make them concrete and believable.

No matter how a performance turns out, if a well-thought-out realistic goal has not been met, sadness and disappointment follow. Disappointment is an experience to be learned from. Avoid linking this feeling to the idea and the feelings of failure. Avoid wallowing in failure, a trap that awaits you if you have set your heart too much on winning. Forgive yourself for not doing as well as you hoped and learn from the experience. Continue to accept yourself as an athlete who did not intentionally perform below expectations. You do not have failures, you only have experiences from which come continuous self-improvement.

Here is another break point in your reading. Take a few minutes to listen and do the next meditation exercise. Exercise 4 on Commitment or Exercise 5 on Confidence would be appropriate at this stage of the program.

● Imaging Goal Achievement

Olympic athletes practice visualizing themselves achieving their goals. Sylvie Bernier, in the last few weeks before she won her gold medal in diving at the 1984 Olympics, spent most of her training time practicing imagery away from the diving pool. She visualized perfect dives in each category. These were her performance goals. A video shows her standing quietly on the board, her eyes closed, focused on her internal images, and then moving smoothly into her dives. In the video, *Visualization, What You See Is What You Get*, she describes how she practiced the images of her outcome goal in each of her sense systems. She *saw* herself walking along the pool to the podium, *heard* the applause of the crowd, and *felt* the medal being placed around her neck.

Greg Louganis, another gold medal winning diver, added a further step in this method. He took time after his good dives to savor, to relish the visceral feelings he had when he knew he had made a perfect dive, whether in practice or in competition. This ensured that the dominant emotions he has when he thinks about his dives are the good feelings of his best dives.

There is no exercise devoted solely to imaging having achieved a goal. Rather, I have included the suggestion in each of the meditation exercises (Exercises 3, 4, 5 and 6.) You are asked to create an image of yourself having achieved the goal of playing with Confidence, or with the easy flowing Concentration of good shot-making.

Be creative in your imaging. Use the video screen in your inner mental room to create and practice the moving image of yourself achieving your goals as in the above examples. Be an observer at first. Watch the video of your success to get in as much detail as possible. Then rerun the video, but this time, be the actor as well. This is easy to do in the image mode and it lets you create these very important visceral images, feeling the joys of success, when you have done well. Remember to add sound to the video to hear the compliments when you make those good shots!

It cannot be stressed too much that positive feedback from the good parts of your golf game is the best foundation for improving your shot-making. Visualize and feel the movements of your good shots, both in practice and on the course. Relish the visceral feelings, the satisfaction, the thrill of a well-played shot. Make these feeling memories the most important emotions attached to the images of your shots.

Goals are there to help you achieve a sense of balance in your life. You must consider important parts of your life when planning goals. Do I really want this goal? What will achieving this goal do to my lifestyle? What will the process of achieving it do to my family, my work, my income, my spiritual health, my self-esteem, my physical health, my important relationships?

● Summary of Chapter Seven

Setting performance goals for yourself is an excellent way to improve your golf game.

● Goals

- start by making short-term goals in putting and chipping, where results come quickly

- increase the difficulty of the goals as needed to meet your ultimate expectations

- motivate yourself by assigning specific dates to achieve your goals

- use simple short-term performance goals when practicing different parts of your game.

● Concrete Example

Set the goal of practicing the PMR exercise once a day for a week prior to a tournament or match. Each time you do the exercise, meditate on the image of yourself playing with just the right level of active relaxation to play well.

● Creative Application

Follow the same preparation the week before an important event in your life, an important presentation, speech, or examination.

Notes on chapter seven

Chapter eight

Problem solving with creative imagery

> *"I can change! You can change!*
> *Everybody can certainly change!"*
>
> *Rocky IV*

> *From the ancient "to be or not to be," to the present*
> *"to become or not to become!"*
>
> *Lars Eric Uneståhl*

● Change a Reaction Habit

Use your Inner Mental Skills to change habitual thoughts or reactions that interfere with your performance. If you say "I always go in the water on this hole" and then replace your regular ball with an old beat-up ball, the negative image is reinforced, as is the expectation that the ball will end up in the water. Or, if your reaction to poor shots is frustration and even anger at yourself, you run the risk that a strong feeling like anger will generate high levels of the messenger molecules that go with the fight or flight response. These excess messenger molecules must go somewhere, and so they are stored in the target cells. From here, they are easily available when needed for the fight or flight response. Subsequently, even minor mistakes can produce strong reactions, reinforcing an undesirable habit. Angry feelings usually remain for several holes, because it takes time for the body to deal with large numbers of these agents.

Fortunately, there is a way to change this kind of habitual response to frustration or anger. My first seminar group of young professionals and top amateurs were concerned about how to handle a disaster, like a badly played hole or a three or four putt green. Golfers say "I lost my concentration" when these errors occur. Together our seminar group worked out a method for surviving such a setback. First, acknowledge the error. This allows you to view the error more objectively, put it out on the table so-to-speak. Second, review in your mind the event from both the mental and physical aspects. Third, replay the shot in your mind as it should have been played. This plays with the memory process because both images vie for long term-memory and neither will win. The result is that the memory of the error is blurred, and the accompanying feelings are muted to a large extent.

Dr. Curt Tribble spoke on Performance Education at the May 1995 Mental Training and Excellence meeting in Ottawa. He was involved with training Cardiovascular Surgeons. Interestingly, these surgeons had a similar problem with handling errors. They became frustrated and angry with themselves when an important stitch was not well-placed. However, they still had to keep going to finish the procedure within a tight time frame. Dr. Tribble taught the Residents to analyze, remember, learn from this, and move on. However, he added an important step: forgiveness. They *forgive* themselves for the error to ease the strong feelings associated with the error. He called this process "Forgive and Remember."

● Forgive, Remember, and Learn

In Exercise 7, I use a simulation to lead you through this process. The scene is this: you have just sculled a chip shot over the green, a shot usually taken for granted. You now face another chip shot, and perhaps your ball is in a lie worse than the first. Normally, at the very least you would feel rattled, at worst disgusted with your ineptness, if you indulged in maligning yourself for poor shots. This exercise combines the original ideas with the new step of forgiveness to provide the following steps:

- acknowledge the error or errors. This makes the error less personal, like putting it out on the table to be examined

- forgive yourself for making the error. This is a simple thought which allows you to look at the error more objectively. (Wouldn't you forgive a friend very quickly for making the same sort of mistake?)

- quickly reflect on the error, looking at both mental and physical aspects. In the image mode, walk through the incident as you would have liked to play the shot. In the meditative state this is a very quick, unobtrusive process because imagery is used

- Remember the experience and benefit from it

● **Here's How**

Instead of allowing this habitual response pattern to develop, follow the above process:

- acknowledge that the performance was not what you had expected

- accept that you do not always make perfect shots

- reflect: were you not quite ready to make the shot? Were you distracted by internal debate, like "I have the wrong club for this shot?" When using imagery, this process is very quick and unobtrusive. No one knows what you are doing when you quietly look at the ground for a moment, then walk purposefully to the next shot. By this time the negative feelings have dissipated and you are ready for the challenge of the next shot

- work into your preparation for the next shot, the feeling of readiness that accompanies your affirmation. For example, "I am committed completely to this club and to this shot"

- finally, replay the shot in your mind as it wants to have been played, confidently creating a good shot. This positive image will interfere with the memory process. The new image will block out the prior image and neither will get into your long-term memory. The method works so well that a word of caution is in order: be sure to write down your score at the time, or you will have difficulty remembering it a few holes later

This reflective process reduces the number of messenger molecules produced when you react to an error and, over time, the level of the stored messenger molecules falls. The habitual self-anger diminishes because it takes a much stronger stimulus to generate a forceful reaction to minor errors.

Notice that this process emphasizes the idea that errors are not the same as failure. Errors and good shots are both experiences to be learned from. We often forget that we learn as much or more from the good things we do as we do from the errors we make. Pay attention to how well you handle and have handled challenges, a major strategy to prevent problems from developing.

Here is another break point in your reading. Take a few minutes now to listen and do Exercise 8 while the ideas are fresh in your mind.

● Recurring Problems in Your Game

Most golfers seem to have at least one problematic hole or shot. Playing a particular tee shot is perhaps the most common situation in which golfer's expect to do poorly. It is the expectation of making a poor shot that is the key. Taking your stance, you feel a little anxious and tense and more aware of hazards. The image focused on is the shot going astray, and more often than not your shot does that, just as you expected would happen. Use your imaging capability to manage this and other similar problems.

Exercise 9 teaches you to use your imaging capability to manage problems, in this example losing your putting stroke. I hope that this common problem can serve as a model to manage other mental problems in your game. Follow the exercise on track nine, but change the directions a little to fit this description. Here is the new procedure:

1. Recall to the screen a scene of the putting problem. This is scene A. Be the actor in the scene and pay particular attention to any body sensation that is a part of it, like tightness in your chest, or gut, or hands. Run it again to focus on the body sensations associated with it. Pick out the most obvious one. Put

the scene away in your memory bank to be recalled later.

2. Now, create a scene in which you are putting very well, how you would like to be putting, that is in your future. Use experiences from the past, even from the practice green. This is scene B. Focus on the body sensations you would have, a sense of confidence in your read of the green, a calmness, concerned only with the present, a feeling of active relaxation, balance, etc. Then shrink this scene to a stamp size and place it in a corner of the screen.

3. Then recall and fill the remainder of the screen with scene A. Make it bright and sharp.

4. Now the important step. Run both scenes at the same time, but rapidly enlarge scene B to fill the screen with bright colourful images, meanwhile letting Scene A fade into the distance and become dull. Open your eyes for a moment or two.

5. Repeat the process five times in each session. Increase the speed in the process each time, as the brain works very fast in the image mode. Open your eyes at the end of scene B to be sure you always go from scene A to scene B.

You should do sets of five in each session and to do several sessions each day. You will notice that it becomes increasingly difficult to recall scene A, or it will become less sharp. Once the experience of not having the problem in real life takes over, it would no longer be necessary to do the exercise. However, problems like this do tend to recur and the reason for paying attention to the body sensations at the start of scene A, is that these sensations can be the first clue that the problem might be recurring. You can then take a moment of your pre-putt routine to run the exercise again a few times, since it takes but a few moments and nobody around you will notice.

Here is another break point in your reading. Listen to and do Exercise 9 while these ideas are fresh in your mind.

Exercise 9 is an NLP Swish technique. This description is an elaboration and follows a Gary Faris example of a skier. He points out that athletes always look to a future performance. Scene B is a future performance. When you listen to exercise 9, you should make scene B a future event.

1. Medical students are taught their interviewing skills using video playback of their history taking with "actor patients." When they view the videotape of the interview afterward, they often laugh at their mistakes and behaviour. Laughing at yourself can spur you on to change. When you are the actor on the TV screen of your imagination you often see the humour in the situation. This helps to change the perception of your performances. The ability to truly laugh at yourself is one of the best ways to dissipate anger associated with your reaction to error.

● Combine the Changed Mental Set with Physical Practice

After doing Exercise 8, take the feeling of confident expectation to your next practice putting session and follow this pattern to reinforce the change. Here is how I go through a putting practice combining the physical with the mental practice:

- Set goals for each practice session and each distance as outlined in Chapter Seven. Review and set higher goals as you improve

- Set three balls about a foot away from the hole and push the balls to the hole to get the feel of the putter head going to the hole, an important move in putting

- Then stroke the balls from the same distance until satisfied with the results. Be sure to keep the putter head going to the hole as before. Set the balls far enough apart so that you have to set up each time as if in a game, rather than bringing the balls to where you are standing

- Repeat the sequence of three balls from 2, 3, 4, and 5 feet. Line up the longer putts. Force yourself to go through your full putting routine, even if just in your mind

- Putting to different targets at different distances sharpens your feel for distance. Pick targets on the green, look at the target for a second or two and check the imaginary line from the target to your putter. Then, trusting in your ability to feel the distance, make the stroke. Focus on making the putter head go along the line chosen, rather than on hitting the ball

- Stop occasionally and review the mental strategy of your putting. Hopefully, you have reviewed these strategies when in your mental room and then used them in your practice putting sessions

● Another Image for Putting

In my putting, I have borrowed an image from martial arts practitioners to help focus less on the ball and more on the distance and the line. When they break boards with their bare hands, they do not focus on the board, but on an image of their hand arriving well below the board. Rather than looking at the ball as I stroke the putt, I imagine the line of the putt underneath the ball, or in front of or behind the ball, and make the putter head go through the ball along that line to the hole.

Notice that you have to soften your eyes, to defocus as

you imagine the putter travelling along the line chosen. An interesting result of this action is that it helps to relax, because you relax the muscle involved in focusing the lens of your eye. Use this action as the trigger to develop the active relaxation needed to putt well. The ball becomes much less important, the images more important. When concentrating on images of the process, you are less interested in what happens to the ball. Of course, this helps to keep your body quiet through the stroke, the undisputed mark of all good putters.

When practicing, beware of fatigue. Do not be afraid to rest, or even to quit when starting to make errors from becoming bored with repetition, or when your back aches from the putting posture. As part of your rest from practice, review the physical and mental routines of your putting. Remember that you want to recall the image of success when putting under stress, like sinking that last putt to make your best score ever.

> **For this is why you play the game: to enjoy yourself, to feel good about your performance, to feel good about yourself. When you expect to feel good about your game, lower scores will follow.**

● Summary of Chapter Eight

Most golfers have one or two recurring problem situations in their game, a shot over water, or out of sand, or a particular tee shot. Each time they are faced with the shot, their anxiety level rises, negative expectations rattle around in their mind, and often a disastrous effort follows.

● Goal

- to practice preventive mental strategies: repeating affirmations quietly to yourself

- to know and to practice methods to re-program the software in your brain

- to change negative expectations to images of successful, well played shots

● Concrete Application

Finding your putting stroke and confidence when in a putting slump. Put your own moving scene on the TV monitor in your mental room and manipulate the scenes as outlined in Exercise 9. Have a friend help. Write a script for her to follow as you go through the exercise.

● Creative Application

Golf is one of the better sport metaphors for life. Many recurring situations in ordinary life are also anxiety producing. Like similar golf situations, each time they recur they are accompanied by a rising feeling of anxiety. Write a script on a minor problem and then follow the method outlined in Exercise 9.

Notes on chapter eight

Chapter nine

Reaching for a best performance

"Peak performers from various fields maintain their child-like qualities!"

Lars Eric Uneståhl

● Playing in the Zone

Peak performances occur in many human activities. The phenomenon has been reported in creative activities, in problem solving, and in performing in the arts. Patients have described to me the peak experiences they had when presenting a term seminar at university, playing volleyball, or while giving a piano concert. This phenomenon has been studied in athletes in all sports, where athletes call it *being in the zone*. Tour player Dave Barr referred to it as like *playing in a glass tunnel* because he was aware of the crowds but unaffected by them. During peak experiences one functions far above one's average level. Abraham Maslow was the first to describe this. He called these experiences "moments of highest fulfillment and happiness."

Surveys of athletes who have experienced a best or peak performance show several common characteristics. These characteristics involve the mind's control over the performance. The mental skills attained by these athletes are also important for your golf game and are well worth emulating:

- **self-image.** Play golf with relaxed self-confidence. Self-confidence is your responsibility. Beware of thinking "I am confident because I am making good shots," because this implies that the only time you play with confidence is when things are going well

- **motivation.** Commit yourself to your standard of play and to your goals. Use imaging to program your goals and to visualize attaining them

- **attitude.** Everything that happens to you teaches you something about yourself. Errors are experiences to learn from, just like the experience of making a good shot

- **mood (your mindset.)** Be optimistic and expect to play well. Practicing optimism can transform a habit of always expecting a bad shot.

● The Ideal Performance Experience

Most of us have had a peak experience, perhaps playing a few holes of golf, or perhaps in another sport or activity altogether. This was an experience when you felt happily absorbed with what you were doing and every task was done automatically with little conscious effort. Afterward, you were aware that something was different, that the performance was well above your usual.

Ideal performance, or best performance, has been studied in many areas of human endeavor, perhaps most extensively in athletic performance. Athletes recognize that they have a different mind set from their ordinary waking state during these experiences. They describe it with phrases like "playing in the zone" or "playing in a cocoon." Dr. Unesthål has interviewed athletes in many sports shortly after their best performances. He noticed how similar these descriptions were to descriptions of the self-hypnotic state. He uses the terms *ideal performance state* or *ideal performance feelings* to distinguish this part of the memory of a peak performance.

Here is a more detailed account of a peak performance in golf to illustrate these ideal performance feelings. Doug Brown was at the time an assistant professional at my club. He described this peak performance to me a few hours after it had occurred. He was still wrapped up in the feelings of it that afternoon after a local pro tour event at Redwood Meadows Golf Club, near Calgary:

"I felt relaxed and confident on awakening and had enough time for a comfortable drive to the course. My rhythm and tempo were nice and smooth on the practice range and green. After the first few holes, I became more aware of the good rhythm in my swing, and that my tempo remained the same in every swing. I felt very confident in my ability to make good contact, and just let my ability work for me.

"Although I was four under par at the turn, and had missed makable putts on the previous two holes, I was not distracted by the score, and just thought about each shot as it came. I was aware that I was pumped up, that the adrenaline was flowing. Even when I went to six under on the 12th hole, my anxiety level never changed, I was very relaxed and calm.

"On the 160 yard 15th, still feeling pumped up and very confident that I was striking the ball well, I decided to go with an eight iron. I don't usually hit an eight iron 160 yards, but I hit this one over the green on the fly into the hazard, and made a double bogey. This had no effect on my feeling of confidence, as I knew I had made a good shot. I remained calm and relaxed with no thought of failure. My pace, my sense of detachment, my rhythm and tempo remained the same throughout the whole day, for a very satisfying round of four under par."

This was a wonderful experience he described. I am sure he dreams about repeating that round. However, reality dictates that no two shots are alike and no two games will ever be the same either. Peak performances are likely associated with the coming together of a number of bodily rhythms, so that one's body is at its absolute peak physically. This is the reason that they appear irregularly, apparently without forewarning, as did Doug's. The state will also disappear suddenly and without warning.

Dr. Unesthål found that athletes who had experienced Inner Mental Training were more likely to have peak performances, and were better able to sustain them when they did occur. These athletes accepted the peak experience without the negative thoughts that golfers often express, that they were playing out of their comfort zone, that playing well was sure to end with the next shot.

● Feeling Memories

There are many pleasant images in the memory of a peak performance: the sound of a putt dropping into the hole, the flight of the ball to the target, the tempo and the fluid motion of a swing repeated over and over. More important to the experience are the associated good feelings, the feeling memories so well described by Doug Brown.

I was introduced to the idea of recalling a peak performance at a hypnosis conference. The speaker asked each person in the audience to develop the altered state and then to access our memory bank to find a peak experience. I was pleasantly surprised to recall a flying experience that I had not thought of for years. It happened during a flight test in Elementary Flying School. The little Tiger Moth seemed a part of me, an extension of myself. I performed each task the instructor gave me the best I had ever done. I hit the slipstream at the end of every turn and loop. The barrel rolls described a perfect circle around the point on the horizon. The landing was so smooth, I thought the wheels started to turn on the grass before touchdown.

Reading this description, you can perhaps pick up on the feelings I still have of the experience. I have had a few peak experiences in golf, and in each instance, the feelings were identical to those of my flying experience.

In the simulation of Exercise 10, you learn to separate out the feeling memories of a peak experience. You can then focus on these feeling images, and project them into a game played out in your mind, a preview of tomorrow's game for example. This exercise may be best reserved for an important game to be played the next day. Bob McArthur, a young professional who was a member of my first series of seminars, used this technique and won most of the Assistant Pro tourna-ments in that year. By itself, this technique will not guar-antee a repeat peak performance, but it will improve your performance because you will expect to play confi-dently. A sustained peak performance has other compo-nents too. You must be in good physical condition and have a good basic swing. You must also have well trained Inner Mental Skills.

Focusing on the very positive feelings associated with a previous ideal performance allows you to expect some errors, but because of your confident feelings, such errors will be looked upon as bad luck or a rub-of-the-green. The errors will then have little or no effect on your con-fidence. This bold-spiritidness is the main aim of this program, what we want in golf and in life.

● Create the Memory of a Future Peak Performance

You will probably have had a peak experience in some activity at some point in your life. In Exercise 10, I ask you to recall such an experience when I lead you through a simulated experience. There may not be a memory of a whole peak experience game in your memory bank, but likely you have played a few holes in the best performance mode. Focus on the associated ideal performance feelings. Run the scene on the TV monitor in your mental room, again being both observer and actor to heighten your memory of the feelings.

The crucial part of the exercise comes next. Create a memory of the future. You are asked to play each shot of an upcoming game on the monitor of your imagination, accompanied with the heightened feeling images of that peak performance. Continue to be both actor and observer to intensify the experience, to make it more real. Run the scene again with the aim of finding an anchor for the feelings. This will provide a fall-back mechanism to help recall your intense peak performance feelings, if they should diminish in real life situations.

Once having done the recorded exercise, practice it on your own without my words. Take as much time as you need. Remember that in the altered mind state you can speed up between shots and play the shots in slow motion to accentuate the feeling memories. If the memory doesn't come the first time you do the exercise, do not be concerned. It may take several sessions, and the recollection may surprise you at another quiet time outside of doing the exercise. When this occurs in the altered state, you will be amazed at how sharp your memory is for these outstanding experiences.

Here is another point in your reading when you can take a break to listen and do the exercise called Peak Experience. Get out disc 2 and do Exercise 10. You can take as much time as you wish to do this exercise by simply carrying on with the experience after the CD ends.

● The Ideal Performance State

As explained earlier, the ideal performance state is very similar to the altered mind state of meditation or hypnosis. Here are some comparable features:

- you will feel totally focused on your shots without trying to do so. It may be like being in a glass tunnel so that you are aware of your surroundings, but the wall around you allows you to concentrate more easily

- you will have a sense that you are watching yourself perform, with no sense of fatigue or discomfort

- you will perceive things differently. For example,

your swing may feel very slow, and you may feel as if you have used no real force in striking the ball, despite the distance and accuracy of the shot. Or, you may perceive that the putt follows the exact path to the hole, that it just cannot miss. These changes in perception help you to expect and to make good shots

- you will experience great joy at the ease with which you are playing. The shots just flow naturally, as if the club is an extension of your body

- you may have difficulty remembering the details of your best shots, but will have little trouble recalling details of the shot that went awry. The importance of this feature is that you must focus on the feelings associated with your best shots, not the details of the shot

In this mind state, the right brain is allowed to dominate the process. Because most of us relate best to the dominant left brain system of control, this alternate way of working takes time and energy to learn. We are not used to allowing effortless control. This is the key, the mind-set for good performance.

The Inner Mental Training program of *Golf: The Mind-Body Connection* provides a structured, systematic method to learn the effortless control of good performance. A peak performance may happen to you only occasionally, but when you experience one, you will now have the skills to keep it going.

Notes on chapter nine

● Summary of Chapter Nine

Peak experiences occur in all walks of life. Golfers and other athletes say they "play in the zone." When asked specific questions about the experience, they relate feelings and perceptions very similar to those observations of people who have experienced the self-hypnotic state.

● Goals

- to become practiced in your imagery capabilities
- to use the altered state to recall the images of a prior peak experience
- to use creative imagery to separate out the feelings of confidence, of easy flowing concentration, of trust in your capabilities

● Concrete Application

Play an important upcoming match or tournament in your mind. Play each shot with those wonderful feeling memories of the prior Peak Experience.

● Creative Application

Transfer the images of an experience in one part of your life to another. For example, if a peak experience happened during a presentation at a meeting, then use the images in a memory of this event and play a future game with these feelings attached. Or vice versa!

Notes on chapter nine

A p p e n d i x   o n e

R e c o r d i n g   y o u r
m e n t a l   s t r a t e g i e s

*"Each time you play a round of golf, you should use it
to indicate the relative strengths and weaknesses of
your game."*

Dr. Bob Rotella

● Making Notes of Your Progress

Start a log book on Inner Mental Training on the same
day you start the exercises. A log book can be a simple
2"x 4" ring bound booklet that you can carry in your
pocket to be easily available, particularly when you use it
at practice. A line or two on your first experience with
self-hypnosis can be about the experience itself: Were
the images sharp? Did the garden scene fit a prior experience that you have had? (When I describe it on the compact disc, I have a combination of two public gardens in
my mind.) Were you able to hear sounds in the scene

clearly? (Interestingly, only about 10 percent of the population list hearing as their favourite sense system. The majority are visualizers.)

When practicing imagery it is important to exercise all the senses no matter which one you favor, because the more details in the image the more you heighten the imagery experience. In the PMR exercise, for example, if you find difficulty in feeling the muscles on the top of the forearm when you pull one hand back, the tendons might feel tight rather than the muscles. Note this. Or, use your free hand to feel the difference in firmness in these muscles as they work to bend the hand backward at the wrist, and make a note of this. If you find a sequence that suits you better than mine, make a more detailed note of this sequence and make the exercise your own.

● Recording Inner Mental Skills Activity

When you use these skills in your games, make notes on the mental strategies used. Did you follow your pre-shot routine? Did you play the shot in a relaxed, confident manner? Were you committed to the club you chose? These are some issues to make note of as you pay attention to the good holes, and the good shots. This is a good way to start: focus on the positive mental strategies used in your games. Avoid focusing exclusively on the errors made to learn from your mistakes. When you pay attention to the good shots, you will find that there were many enjoyable moments in the game. This emphasis puts your golf into perspective even if many of your shots do not meet your expectations.

As you become more practiced at this, make the observations more specific. For example, what strategies worked well? How did you handle distractions? Were you able to maintain a good tempo? Were you close to your ideal active relaxation level? Were some shots played when you were too relaxed, when in the relaxation part of your pre-shot routine and not quite ready to make the shot? Create strategies to get around the problems encountered. If your visual images are not sharp, you might imagine using a long lens camera to magnify and sharpen the images. If you have a favourite image system, find images in the other systems that appeal to you too. On some days, I find that visualizing a shot is easier, even though my kinesthetic sense of feeling the swing is my preferred image system. In any case, do not neglect your less favoured image systems, because they just might be important in different circumstances, or on a different course.

All golfers make mental notes, a mental diary, of their practice sessions and their games. Many know how many greens they hit and most know how many putts they took in the round. However, the process of writing a diary makes analysis more thorough and more objective. It also enhances the positive feelings, because you focus on improving smaller segments of your game. If you do not golf every day, a diary provides continuity. If you include practice sessions in the diary, the swing thoughts and routines you develop on the practice fairway transfer more easily to the course.

● The Manzer Model Diary

A friend, Len Brayton, keeps a golf diary by asking himself, "What specific shot made me miss the green in regulation[1] figures?" This is easy for Len, since it means

1. Regulation is the way par for the hole is divided. That is, 3 shots to the green and 2 putts for a par 5 hole. That is why modern courses have several tees, moving them forward for higher handicap golfers. If you are in this latter category, regulation figures for you may be 4 or 5 strokes to reach the green on a par 5 hole. All scorecards have a column (or row) labelled men's handicap, or lady's handicap. The figures for each hole (from

one or two entries per game! Another friend, Carson Manzer, a 16 handicapper, has learned that forcing himself to ask this same question makes for a better analysis of the hole.

After each game Carson summarizes the shots that caused him to miss greens in regulation figures. He uses an ordinary course scorecard for the nine categories he requires. Since most cards do not have enough empty rows (or columns) for the nine categories, he over-writes those used for other purposes. For clarity, Figure 3 is a scorecard with unlabelled rows and columns. A similar blank card appears on page 162, which you may photocopy and fold inside the scorecard.

The nine categories to be recorded in the Manzer model, together with his shorthand symbol in brackets to indicate the column (or row), are:

- Gross score

- Drives (D)

- Fairway woods (FW)

1 to 18) indicate the rated difficulty for that hole. If your handicap is 24, you are allowed 2 strokes on all those holes rated 6 and under and 1 stroke for the remainder. That is, the course par for you is 24 strokes above the rated par for the course. The system allows you to play a match with any other player giving or taking strokes according to your handicaps.

- Full iron shots (I)

- Pitches, less than a full iron shot (P)

- Chips, less than a pitch, and either to the green or out of trouble to the fairway (CH)

- Sand shots from green-side bunkers only (S)

- Putts (these do not require a symbol and are recorded in the handicap row)

- Why? Circle the shot that was responsible for the green not reached in regulation figures.

The shorthand symbols used in the recording of shots are:

0	a circle around the hole number is a green reached in regulation
✓	a check-mark for a satisfactory shot
L	a shot Left, a pull or hook
R	a shot Right, a push or slice
S	a shot Short of target
O	over the target, (instead of long)

WHY... In the "WHY" column, combine symbols to indicate the shot that caused the missed green. DR is a Drive sliced or pushed Right.

Here are a few conventions to help simplify record keeping:

Figure 3. Model game score card   (See Specimen Game Card on page 141 to copy for your own use.)

HOLE NO.	①	②	③	④	⑤	⑥	⑦	⑧	⑨	OUT	⑩	⑪	⑫	⑬	⑭	⑮	⑯	⑰	⑱	IN	PAR	GH: 5 / GOOD SHOTS
YARDAGE	524	389	373	381	399	307	144	389	188		374	420	376	149	511	197	300	388	530			
PAR	5	4	4	4	4	4	3	4	3	35	4	4	4	3	5	3	4	4	5	36	71	
SCORE	5	5	5	5	7	5	2	5	4	43	5	6	4	3	7	5	5	5	5	45	88	
DRIVES	✓	✓	R	✓	R	✓		R			✓	S	✓		L	R	✓	✓	✓			9 OF 16
F. WOODS	✓	R	R	S	R			S				L	✓		S		S		S			3 of 8
IRONS	✓		R		O	L	✓				✓		✓	✓	S		✓	✓				6 of 12
PITCH		✓			O			✓			✓					✓			✓			5 OF 6
CHIPS					✓✓	✓	✓									✓						6 OF 7
SAND SHOTS																						1 OF 3
WHY GREEN MISSED		FR	DR	IR	DR	IL		DR	DS	IO	IO	DS			FS	DR	IS		FS			35 GOOD SHOTS
PUTTS	2	2	2	2	2	2	1	2	2	17	2	2	2	2	3	2	2	3	1	19	36	

- if an iron is used from the tee, record this as an iron shot

- fairway bunker shots are fairway shots

- write penalty strokes in the same column as putts

- if you do not hit the ball long, three shots to the green for a long par four hole may be the figure you have in mind when you ask yourself whether you reached the green in regulation.

● Analyzing the Information

Look at Figure 3. For each hole, there is a symbol for each shot, and with the putts, this total is your score for that hole. For hole number 1, there are three check marks and two putts. Some judgment is necessary. For example, on holes 5 and 15, the player had to chip out from trees and he played these shots well. On hole 14, his drive was in the rough, but since he had a good lie he should have made a good fairway wood shot. This latter shot is the one that prevented him from reaching the green in regulation figures. A detailed putting record can be added by using the same ideas as in the fairway game, e.g., symbols such as LL for left and long, or PR for pin high but right. An extra row is added to the model form for this purpose.

The following is a natural grouping of the three components of any golf score:

- The fairway game. This is the sum of the drives, fairway wood shots and iron shots.
- The short game: pitches, chips and sand shots.
- The putting game.

Carson concerns himself with the number of greens hit in regulation (GH) and with his net field score (NFS.) The NFS is the difference between the gross score and the sum of putts plus penalty strokes. (Penalty shots add to the gross score but not to the net field score.)

Carson has a handicap of 16 and he aims for an NFS of under 50. In this game, (Figure 3) his gross score was 88. He used 36 putts giving him an NFS of 52, which did not meet this goal.

However, he listed 35 of his shots as good shots, a ratio of 35:52, or 70 percent. His putting game could improve, or perhaps he could be more selective in what he considers to be a good chip. He might set a goal of playing his short game shots to within five feet of the hole, 90 percent of the time. This would better his putting game as he would have a chance at more one putt greens.

Figure 4 is the summary of why the greens were missed. (Carson is a right-handed golfer):

	Drives	FW	I	Tot	Analysis of the game
Left	0	0	1	1	Of the 13 greens missed: 6 were due to shots to the right, 4 of which were woods. 5 shots were short or topped wood shots. There was no pattern to the missed iron shots.
Right	4	1	1	6	
Short	2	2	1	5	
Over	0	0	1	1	
Totals	6	3	4	13	

A review of several game summaries, like this example, defines the problems to take to the practice fairway or to your instructor for help. As an example from this one game of Carson's, he wants to correct his tendency to slice or push his shots. This is an intermediate goal toward his performance goal of increasing the number of greens he hits in regulation.

Besides the summary of greens missed, use the card to analyze the game in all categories and record all the ratios. One example in this game is that there were 35 good shots out of the total of 52 shots. Carson also had 4 good pitch shots out of 6 tries and 6 good chips out of 7 tries. I use Carson's system as an *aide mémoire* for my mental strategies because it is too easy to forget the mental associations of the shots even shortly after a game. I write a narrative diary after a game or a practice session. The model has proven to be very useful to help highlight the shots needing analysis and the parts of my game needing practice.

When we analyze performance, we have to analyze the errors we made. Beware of the trap of moving from "what is wrong with my game" to "there is something wrong with me." Like good shots, learn from errant shots. Never, ever think of them as failures. It is too easy to generalize with such a powerful word, to think of yourself as a failure because you have made an error.

Do take the next step and work on the lessons learned from analyzing your games. Otherwise the effort is wasted and this may turn you against keeping records of your games before seeing the benefits of a diary.

Notes on appendix one

Appendix two

Is all this new? Theoretical considerations

● Left and Right Brain

Athletes commonly say "the less you think, the better you perform," because you use your sequentially analytic left brain less and your intuitively creative right brain more. Golfers have to avoid "paralysis by analysis" in their pre-shot routine. With practice, you will learn to trust your right brain functions and balance them with your left brain activities. The best human performances occur when the functions of both sides of the brain are integrated and coordinated. For example, EEG studies of a concert violinist showed that both sides of his brain were very active during a performance. The brain activity of his audience was mainly on the right side.

Studies of right and left brain function form the theoretical background for this program. Left brain activity is the dominant mode in our everyday work. We analyze and use sequential logic to solve problems. When we hit a block we switch to right brain activity. For example, we "sleep on the problem," or just take a break. The right brain is more involved with creativity, nonverbal understanding, kinesthetic and spatial images and modeling; feel, touch, and tempo are also located here. This is not entirely clearcut as many functions and activities are represented on both sides of the brain. It is a very complicated organ indeed. Right brain involvement shows up on the electroencephalogram (EEG): we can see increased right brain activity during the altered states of hypnosis and meditation. (See figure 1, p61)

● Ultradian Rhythms

Dr. Milton Erickson, a prominent modern psychotherapist, noticed that most people slip into trances often throughout the day. He called these episodes "common everyday trances" and incorporated them into his therapy sessions. We are all familiar with the faraway look of students during a lecture, or of staring into space for a few minutes during your work. Dr. Ernest Rossi studied this idea: he had his patients record their daily activities in detail. His studies confirm that we have a Basic Rest Activity Cycle, BRAC for short. These cycles have a period ranging from 90 to 120 minutes. During these daydream times, we shift to right brain dominance. It seems that the brain needs a rest from its usual control activity and shifts body systems into their maintenance mode for a time. This maintenance mode is manifested by an increase in intestinal and urinary activity; respiratory changes are indicated by a yawn or a sigh; the heart-rate slows and the skin warms. It is "take a break" time when you get up and move around, go to the bathroom or have a drink, or do something to feel relaxed. Most of us are not aware of these cycles and if there is much stimulation in our environment, it is easy to ignore the signals.

Researchers call these ultradian rhythms, or cycles that last less than a day, in contrast to circadian rhythms which last about a day like our sleep/wake cycle. Awareness of these rhythms will allow you to recognize the rest period part of your day. This may be the best stress reliever you have. Take a small portion of the rest period to direct your daydreams about your golf game. This will not interfere with the natural benefit of the rejuvination period and will certainly add to your practice time for such things as reviewing your preshot routine or practicing anchors in your imagination.

● Relaxation

Remember, the relaxation that golfers strive for in their shotmaking is not the deep level found in TM, in hypnosis, or in other techniques used for therapeutic ends. Rather, it is an active relaxation in which the muscles that oppose an active muscle have just the right amount of tone to allow that active muscle to function at its best. Leif Janson found that his best archers had this ability in spades. The best athletes in every sport he studied had the same capability as did the best stringed instrument players. By inference, all performers require the ability to establish active relaxation, meaning they require just the right tone in opposing muscles to perform well.

During the 1994 Swedish Master's tournament Janson took the opportunity to study golfers with different levels of ability. The tracing and graphics of the muscle activity of the extensor muscles of the right forearms of two players are presented in Figures 5 and 5a. The ability of the better golfer to perform with a smooth controlled muscle action is well illustrated in the actual tracings inset in the diagrams. The graphs represent 7 swings of each player. Notice how the better player uses the same force for each swing. In contrast, notice the variability of muscle activity in the player of lesser ability. Notice also that he was satisfied with shots that were made with much unnecessary activity in his opposing muscles.

Janson also found that good golfers are so used to their own technique that they cannot feel, or do not know, what happens in their swing. For example, he reported that some of these good players had nearly 100 percent of their maximum voluntary isometric contraction (MVC) at the top of their backswing. They gripped the club very hard at this point in their swing. Other players did this at the point of ball-strike. Both habits would tend to produce errant shots. Janson used biofeedback to teach these players to smooth out this unnecessary muscle activity with excellent results. The tour players concerned were gratified with the results too!

Can this skill be taught? For a professional athlete looking for the edge he needs to win, biofeedback technology would be cost effective. Swedish researchers used the well known PMR because it is always available to athletes and is the best method for basic training in this skill. They found that it took an adult 4 weeks of twice daily sessions of PMR to learn the correct level of relaxation in those muscle groups important to their sport. Dedicated athletes were highly motivated, putting in 20 minute sessions twice daily until they mastered this muscle control.

Results of this simple exercise are impressive. I can vouch for its effectiveness in my golf game and in my skiing. I put in a month of daily PMR sessions before the skiing season and I believe I am skiing with more relaxed, controlled turns than ever before. Moreover, I no longer have the painful calf muscle that used to plague me for several days after a day's skiing. I believe my calf muscles are relaxed because I no longer try to hold on to my boot with my toes during turns.

Figure 5. This graph is of 7 shots of Ian Woosnam. The bars show the muscle activity of his extensor muscles during his swings. The right hand bar is his grip pressure at the start, the second bar at ball strike. Grip pressure is measured as a percentage of the Maximum Voluntary Contraction of these muscles. The inset is the Electromyographic (EMG) tracing of one swing. There is no unnecessary muscle activity in his take-away nor in his down-swing, so there are only two bars shown. The numbers below the bars indicate his estimate of the outcome of the shots, 5 being the best. Janson found Woosnam's swing to be the smoothest and most accurate he tested.

Figure 5

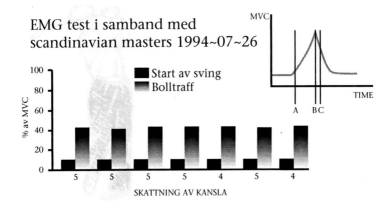

Figure 5a. This graph is that of a lesser skilled player. The middle bar shows the "unwished for" muscle activity during his take-away and at the top of his back-swing. The EMG tracing indicates this extra activity throughout his swing. (Janson calls this "Jack" in the graph.) Notice the variability of the grip pressure throughout his swing. This player accepts this extra muscle activity as a normal part of his swing, judging from his assessment of the outcome of each shot. Janson found that some good players have 100 percent of their MVC at the top of the back-swing and at ball strike and are unaware of this because they are so used to their technique.

(The graphs in these figures are reprinted with permission of Leif Janson from his studies made at the Swedish Masters Tournament July 26, 1994. He published them in his book Avspänd Teknik.)

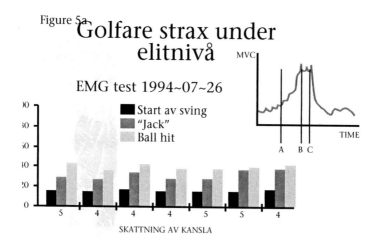

Figure 5a.

● Historical Considerations

The phenomena of the altered state has always been a part of human existence. The ancients incorporated it into their prayer rituals and healing practices. This can even be found in cultures comparatively untouched by civilization. In eighteenth-century Europe there was a strong tradition of faith healing and many physicians and priests were involved in its use. An Austrian physician named Franz Anton Mesmer (1734 - 1815), showed that he could cure patients using his method just as well as a famous faith healer who claimed miracle cures using the exorcism rite. (There was a strong belief in possession by good and bad spirits at that time. The bad spirits caused illness.)

Mesmer lived at the beginning of the Age of Enlightenment, when men thought that science would eventually explain all of the phenomena of the natural world. Magnetism had been discovered and Mesmer theorized that his technique tapped into this force to cure illness. He called this use of magnetism animal magnetism, the first cohesive theory to explain the phenomena in what we now call hypnosis.

In Mesmer's clinics the patients held onto metal rods

placed in water containing iron filings. He would appear in flowing purple robes and make passes over the patients with his hands. Some cures did occur and Mesmer and his followers soon became popular, despite vigorous opposition from the conservative Medical Faculty in Paris. The Royal Society of Science set up a Commission of Inquiry headed by Benjamin Franklin, who was then American ambassador to France. The inquiry disproved the theory of animal magnetism but did not dispute the cures, saying only that the cures were due to the influence of the patient's imagination. Mesmer became disenchanted with the Medical Faculty's stubbornness in refusing even to consider his theories, and never achieved his dream of being accepted by his physician peers. He left Paris and retired from medicine.

● Mesmerism and Other Theories

Physicians across Europe continued to use the technique because it could be used for pain relief during surgery. James Esdaile (1808 - 1868), a surgeon working with the East India Company, reported using mesmerism as the only anesthetic in over one thousand surgical operations. Of these, 350 were major procedures. Not only were the operations successful, but both the morbidity rate (infections and blood loss) and the mortality rate were less than half those expected, despite the primitive conditions. He continued this practice with equal success when he returned to Britain. Ether and then chloroform became available in the 1840s, causing interest in using mesmerism for surgical anesthesia to decline.

Physicians of that time were puzzled by patients who were deeply mesmerized and seemingly without pain during surgical procedures. James Braid (1795 - 1860), an eye surgeon in Scotland, theorized that it was related to sleep and coined the word hypnosis, feeling that it was a type of nervous sleep (from *hypnos,* the Greek word for sleep.) He introduced the technique in which the patient focused on a watch waving like a pendulum to enter the mesmeric state.

Later in the century, Jean Martin Charcot (1825 - 1893), a leading neurologist in Paris, linked hypnosis to hysteria, a disease state. Although this theory about hypnosis was more acceptable to the scientific community, it was soon discarded. He was working with institutionalized mental patients, not a representative cross-section of people. Some of these patients may have had hysterical symptoms and many had a self-interest in obeying Dr. Charcot, since he was also head of the hospital.

Unlike Charcot's theory, a country doctor named August Ambrose Liébault (1823 - 1904), and a city of Nancy neurologist, Hippolyte Bernheim (1840 - 1919), developed the theory that hypnosis was connected to a person's suggestibility. A colleague, Emile Coué (1856 - 1926), astutely observed that to be effective, an instruction had to become a self-suggestion. These three practitioners dealt with the general population and well recognized the variability in their patients' capability to use these mental skills. Coué is responsible for the generic self-suggestion, "every day in every way, I am better and better." Affirmations, like those in this program, are based on this idea.

● Modern ideas

In World War II, psychiatrists used hypnosis to treat battle fatigue because they saw a link between the mental state of these soldiers and the dissociation theory of Dr. Pierre Janet (1859 - 1947), Charcot's successor in

Paris. (Dissociation means that we have the ability to be in two or more places at once through our imaging capability. Danny Kaye's Walter Mitty is an excellent comedy on this theme.) Dentists used hypnosis for pain control when local anesthetic supplies ran out during that war. Since then, there has been a surge of interest and research in hypnosis, particularly relating to the mind-body connection.

How does the mind affect the immune system? Dr. Karen Olness, a pediatric immunologist, has shown that children can increase the immune protein material (some of these proteins are antibodies) in their saliva. Three groups of children were shown a movie of how the immune system works. The first group saw only the movie. The second group were asked to meditate only. The experimental group of children "directed their dreams," creating appropriate suggestions to increase the amount of immune protein in their saliva. They did so to levels well above the two control groups. Dr. Olness called this ability *cyberphysiologic control* (cyber from the Greek kybernetes, meaning to steer.) She recently reported (Frontiers of Hypnosis, Banff, May 1995) that a follow-up study in Australia proved the effectiveness of this strategy. School children, taught how to increase immune proteins in their saliva, had a much lower incidence of respiratory infections during the "colds season," shown by fewer absences from school.

Dr. Uneståhl noticed that the behavior and attitudes athletes develop during a peak performance are also well developed in patients who cope best with serious illness. He called this behavior the "ideal health state." One implication of this observation is that everyone can learn these skills. This implies that the Inner Mental Skills we associate with sport can enhance health, improve education, help with business success and can be applied to the workplace. In Sweden the spread of mental training into other fields is already well advanced. For example, Swedish Police find the training helpful in managing the potentially difficult situations they encounter.

● **Persuasion and the placebo effect**

A brief explanation of how and why we pay attention to a stimulus from our surroundings may help you understand this process. It is one explanation of the process of concentration. After a stimulus hits the sense organ a signal is generated and proceeds through the brain where it interacts with memories and their associated feelings. These modify the image created by the stimulus. It is the strength of the signal when it reaches the cerebral cortex, and therefore your awareness, which decides the attention you give it. This awareness includes the feelings associated with the images. A person who has a phobia to snakes has a rush of fearful feelings at the sight of a snake, so he pays a great deal of attention to that snake!

Feedback from a memory of a previous experience can increase the strength of the signal if the associated emotions are there. If you focus on the negative images, "I've missed short putts like this one before," then you cannot concentrate on the positive image of making the putt. Practicing the positive imagery related to putting like, "I've made hundreds of putts like this one," will reinforce your confidence and so your ability to concentrate on that putt. A shot out of sand may be unnecessarily difficult if your image of this shot is one of driving the club through the sand with great effort. You will tend to focus on the effort and likely spoil the shot. Changing this image to one of allowing the club to slide through the sand under the ball with little effort produces a positive change in both attitude and performance.

Once we learn to reprogram the "software" in our brains like this, we can use this skill in positive ways. We can *persuade* ourselves to be more positive in performance. We can *persuade* ourselves to increase the antibodies in our saliva to combat the infectious agents that most often enter through the mouth. We can also *persuade* ourselves to modify our perception of pain, a useful skill even with modern medical technology.

A surgeon friend with a peptic ulcer noticed that when he wakened at night with ulcer pain, often the pain would disappear before he took his antacid. The expectation of pain relief was as important as the antacid. This phenomenon is called the *placebo effect*, usually described as the same effect being produced with a sugar pill as with the real thing. I believe that when you use your Inner Mental Skills you tap into this complex placebo phenomenon. We all experience the placebo effect. Up to 60 percent of the effect of any pill can be the result of the placebo effect. Researchers go to great lengths to determine how much of the effect of a new medication is due to this effect.

George Peper, in his lead editorial of the August 1996 Golf Magazine, discusses "the 45-day rule." This rule states that you can have a 45-day honeymoon with a new golf club, but the magic will not last forever because of the placebo effect. That is, you hit the ball longer because you believe the club is better, just as you believe the sugar pill is the real thing. The 45-day rule can be broken. The placebo effect can last as long as you want it to when you use your Inner Mental Skills and learn to trust yourself to play well.

A complete explanation of what happens during the hypnotic or meditative state is not yet available. An interesting newer idea is that it belongs with the art of persuasion. The literature on this includes that of sales ability and the art of rhetoric. Alan Scheflin, a lawyer who studies hypnosis from his legal background, spoke of this idea in Banff at the 1995 conference, Frontiers of Hypnosis.

When you use self-suggestion you are using a form of persuasion. When you make suggestions that evoke images like seeing and feeling yourself achieving your goals, you

**are using your total mind. This is a
very powerful positive persuasive
force for good in your life as well as
in your golf game.**

Notes on appendix two

B i b l i o g r a p h y
a n d   r e s o u r c e s

Benson, Herbert. (1984) *Beyond the Relaxation Response.* New York: Berkley Books Edition, Times Books. (An excellent book, and a good introduction to the ideas of this program.)

Botterill Lifestyles. (1986) *Visualization, What You See Is What You Get,* (Videotape.) The Coaching Association of Canada. (An excellent presentation for coaches on visualization in a variety of sports. Golf is not mentioned as they focus on Olympic athletes.)

Cohn, Patrick J. (1991) "An Exploratory Study on Peak Performance in Golf." *The Sport Psychologist,* 5-14.

Enhager, Kjell and Samantha Wallace. (1991) *Quantum Golf.* Warner Books, Inc., New York. (Written in the manner of Golf in the Kingdom, but from the perspective of the Quantum Theories of Depak Chopra.)

Goleman, D., Gurin J. (Eds.) (1993) *Mind Body Medicine.* How to Use Your Mind for Better Health. Consumer Reports Books. (Multiple Authored essays on every aspect of health. You might notice the similarities rather than the differences between the various techniques described. [between guided imagery and hypnosis, for example].)

Grinder John, Brander Richard. (1981) *Trance-formations*. Real People Press, Moab UT. (This, and several other books by these authors, is the original introduction to Neuro-Linguistic Programming. The second problem solving exercise is an example of one such technique.)

Hall, E.G, Hardy, C.J. (1981) "Using the Right Brain in Sport." In *New Paths to Sport Learning*, J. Salmella, J. Parkington and T. Orlick, Eds. Ottawa : Coaching Associ ation of Canada. (This article surveys the theory as applied to sport. There are several good articles in this manual , including an early one by Uneståhl.)

Haltain, Arnold. (1908) *The Mystery of Golf*. Applewood Books, Cambridge/Boston. (Reprinted in 1965 and 1986 with a foreword by Herbert Warren Wind. "… what Izaak Walton's "The Compleat Angler" is to books on fishing,… the Mystery of Golf is to books on golf.)

Hogan, Charles. (1988) *Nice Shot*. (Video and booklet.) Sports Enhancement Associates, Columbia SC.

Jensen, Peter. (1993) *Golfer's Inside Edge*. (Audio Tape Presentation.) Performance Coaching Inc. Rockwood, ON.

Loehr, James E. (1994) *The New Toughness Training for Sports*. Penguin Books USA, New York, NY. (The author's extensive experience with high performance athletes, including tour players, provides the basis of programming yourself for competition. His daily diary model is very comprehensive.)

Mackenzie, Marlin M.(1990) *Golf The Mind Game*. Dell Publishing, New York, NY. (A master practitioner of Neuro-Linguistic Programming, he outlines many NLP techniques for solving golf problems.)

Miller, John."One Day Wonders." *Golf Illustrated*, October 1990. (He talks about "the little voice that talks to me." This is very reminiscent of the inner coach that I talk of in this program.)

Murphy, Michael. (1972) *Golf in the Kingdom*. New York: Viking Press. (This classic has been recently re-released. A must book for the serious and the not so serious golfer interested in the mind and human performance. He speaks through the mythical Scottish pro, Shivas Irons.)

Olness K., Culbert T., Uden D. "Self Regulation of Salivary Immunoglobulin A by Children." *Pediatrics*, Vol 83, No 1, January, 1989. (An excellent article on the ability of the mind to affect the immune system.)

Orlick, Terry. (1986.) *Psyching for Sport*. Champaign, IL: Leisure Press. (Organiser of the 1995 World Congress on Mental Training and Excellence in Ottawa, he is an internationally renowned writer and speaker on mental preparation for sport. His work with Olympic athletes is the subject of this book.)

Peper, George. "Tee Dance." *Golf Magazine*, August 1996. (This editorial discusses the placebo effect associated with owning a new club that works well for you: the 45-day rule. It works because the player believes that it is better. The effect lasts about 6 weeks.)

Price, Charles. "What is a Player?" *Golf Digest*, April 1984. (A description of a person who plays the game of golf versus one who is a golfer. Perhaps we should all aspire to the description of a player that Price writes about.)

Pulos, Lee. (1990) *Beyond Hypnosis*. San Francisco & Vancouver, Omega Press. (He has a long experience consulting with professional hockey and football players as well as Olympians. He has also studied healing practices in cultures untouched by Western ideas. He blends the practical with the theoretical to point toward the "Future Mind," his view of the potential of the human mind in all aspects of life.)

Rossi Ernest L. (1991) *The Twenty Minute Break: the Ultradian Healing Response*. Los Angeles: Jeremy Tarcher. (A practical guide to the basic activity rest cycle and its every day applications.)

Rotella, Bob, Cullen Bob. (1995) *Golf is Not a Game of Perfect*. New York, NY. Simon & Schuster. (An excellent book written in a conversational manner with anecdotes and experiences from tour players on mental preparation for golf. He has a straightforward approach to attitudes and behaviours for playing better golf.)

Rubenstein, Lorne. (1996) "Different Strokes." *Senior Golfer*, August 1996: 42 - 49. (He has written many articles on Moe Norman. This one includes Moe's Musings, pithy sayings from Moe. The quote in Chapter Five is from this article.)

Scheflin, Alan W. "The Current Assaults on Hypnosis and Therapy." Presentation at Frontiers of Hypnosis Conference, Banff, May 1995. (He talked about the art of persuasion in this presentation.)

Tribble, Curt and Newberg, Doug: "Dealing with Sub-optimal Outcomes." Presentation at Mental Training and Excellence Conference, Ottawa, May 1995. (I learned the idea of forgiving oneself for errors from their talk on Performance Education in graduate medical education.)

Uneståhl, Lars Eric (Ed.)(1986) *Contemporary Sport Psychology*, Proceedings of the VI World Congress in Sport Psychology. Örebro, Sweden. Veje Publishing Inc. (Dr. Uneståhl is a world renowned authority on mental training. He is a founding faculty member of the Scandinavian International University in Örebro Sweden, and is President of the International Society for Mental Training. The second world congress of the society was held in Ottawa in May of 1995.)

Uneståhl, Lars Eric." Mental Skills for Sport and Life." Paper given at the VII World Congress in Sport Psychology, Singapore, August, 1989. (This paper outlines the Swedish experience with Inner Mental Training and the research background for the programs. This and other pamphlets are available from Dr. Uneståhl at The Scandinavian International University, P.O. Box 3085, S-70003, Örebro, Sweden.)

Uneståhl, Lars Eric, Bundsen, Pavel. (1996) "Neuro-Biochemical Mechanisms and Psycho-Physical Consequences." *Hypnos*, XXIII, No 3: 148 - 156. (A Swedish/Russian study of EEG tracings during mental training. Athletes, students of all ages and health workers were studied.)

Williams, Jean M. (Ed), (1986) *Applied Sport Psychology*. Palo Alto, CA: Mayfield Publishing Company. (Nideffer, an expert on concentration in sport, has an excellent chapter in this book. Ravizza's chapter on peak performance is also good. Uneståhl has a chapter on his early experience on hypnosis in sport.)

I n d e x

Specimen model game score-card for photocopying.

HOLE NO.	1	2	3	4	5	6	7	8	9	10	11	12	13	14	15	16	17	18			GH:
YARDAGE																					
PAR																					
SCORE																					
DRIVES																					
F. WOODS																					
IRONS																					
PITCH																					
CHIPS																					
SAND SHOTS																					
WHY GREEN MISSED																					
PUTTS																					

Special Notes

S p e c i a l   N o t e s

Special Notes

Special Notes

For further information

Dr. Saunders can be contacted at:

phone: (403) 240-3036

fax: (403) 206-0695

105 Sierra Morena Terrace SW

Calgary, Alberta, Canada T3H 3A2

What others are saying about the program:

"Dr. Saunders' program will help people in all sports. Unlike squash or tennis, the golfer has more time to think between shots, . . . I believe that the program can be useful for all golfers, from the novices to the top pros on the PGA tour."

Howard Broun, former New Zealand Davis Cup player, New Zealand Squash Champion and world-ranked player, World "Over 35" Squash Champion, and now a scratch golfer.

"Dr. Saunders' program not only points out the skills that are necessary in developing a strong mental approach to the game of golf, it also gives you a system in how to put it into practice. I particularly like the chapters on *Inner Mental Training* and *Problem Solving with Creative Imagery.* The whole book is full of extremely valuable information that serious golfers can put to excellent use."

Don Price, Director of Golf, Glencoe Golf & Country Club

"The best shots you hit signify your physical ability. How often you hit these shots in a variety of situations relates to your mental ability. Dr. Saunders program will enhance the connection of these abilities, resulting in a greater likelihood of hitting your best shots in any situation."

Ron Laugher, Head Professional, Priddis Greens Golf & Country Club

Tom Saunders, M.D., has merged his life's work as a physician with his life's pleasure, golf. As a doctor, he enjoyed many years teaching self-hypnosis to patients. As a professor, he taught medical students and trainees in Family Medicine how to use the techniques to help their patients manage medical problems. Noticing the similarity of self-hypnosis to mental training programs for Olympians led him to try the techniques for his own game. When he improved, he taught the techniques to golfers and other athletes helping them reach their potential. This experience became the basis of this program, *Golf: The Mind Body Connection.*

A Professor Emeritus at the University of Calgary, Dr. Saunders is a graduate of McGill University with an M.A. in medical education from Michigan State University. He plays to a 12 handicap.